THE
SHATTERED
SELF

THE SHATTERED SELF

E.T.A. Hoffmann's Tragic Vision

Horst S. Daemmrich
Wayne State University

WAYNE STATE UNIVERSITY PRESS
Detroit 1973

Copyright © 1973 by Wayne State University Press, Detroit, Michigan 48202.
All rights are reserved. No part of this book may be reproduced
without formal permission.

Published simultaneously in Canada by the Copp Clark Publishing Company
517 Wellington Street, West Toronto 2B, Canada.

Library of Congress Catalog Card Number
International Standard Book Number

Library of Congress Cataloging in Publication Data

Daemmrich, Horst S   1930–
  The shattered self.

  Bibliography: p. 131
  1. Hoffmann, Ernst Theodor Amadeus, 1776–1822.
I. Title.
PT2361.Z5D28 1973   833'.6   73-1490
ISBN 0-8143-1493-7

O sieh doch nur die Dämonen ihre Krallenfäuste
ausstrecken, dich hinabzureissen in den Orkus!

E.T.A. Hoffmann

contents

preface 9

1

HOFFMANN, THE MAN AND HIS TIME
13

2

A NEW LOOK AT HOFFMANN
19

3

SELF-REALIZATION AND SELF-TRANSCENDENCE
25

4

STRUGGLE FOR A NEW VISION OR THE INFERNAL CIRCLE
39

5

LEBENSANGST AND FAILURE
47

THE STRANGE FAIRYLAND
55

7

VISIONS OF COMPULSION AND DEATH—THE INFERNAL FAIRY TALES
73

8

THE SHATTERED SELF
93

9

THE GRAND DESIGN AND GERMAN PESSIMISM
111

notes 119

bibliography 131

index 139

preface

HOFFMANN HAS ALWAYS BEEN A FAVORITE German author in Europe, Canada, and the United States. Interest by
critics in his stories has increased considerably in recent
times. After a brief descriptive introduction which places
Hoffmann in the historical context of his age and an outline
of main trends in critical appraisals of his achievement, I
shall analyze the major themes and motifs in his work. The
study will show that they form a dynamic structural pattern
which constitutes the basis for a grand design of man in
search for identity. In his design Hoffmann captured the
struggle between man's yearning for self-transcendence and
the will to self-assertion as well as the clash between visions
of beauty and the atavistic forces of evil. By identifying the
feeling of fear with man's existence and the image of the
cage with the structure of the world, Hoffmann portrayed
the disintegration of the individual in a world of uncontrol-

9

led forces. The grand design is of singular importance because it embraces Hoffmann's literary work as a whole and sheds light upon the aesthetic structure of his narratives. The originality of the conception demanded a new artistic technique and a total transformation of old values. Hoffmann recognized the problem and looked into the chaos. But it was left to philosophers to continue his thinking and to modern existentialism to search for a completely new basis for man's existence.

I am indebted to the *Germanic Review* and *Papers on Language and Literature* for permission to include in this study extensively revised material from articles previously published in those journals. I also hope that the conception of a grand design based on dynamic patterns proves useful to critics in studies of other authors.

THE
SHATTERED
SELF

All titles of Hoffmann's works are given in English, once they have been identified in German. Though Hoffmann's best-known works have frequently been translated into English, lesser known tales and his correspondence have not. I have used my translation, so that all references could be made to standard German critical editions which are reliable and easily available.

Abbreviations for references to Hoffmann:

W E.T.A. Hoffmann, *Werke*, ed. Georg Ellinger, 15 vols. (Berlin, 1912).

FN E.T.A. Hoffmann, *Fantasie- und Nachtstücke*, ed. Walter Müller-Seidel (Darmstadt, 1966).

El E.T.A. Hoffmann, *Die Elixiere des Teufels*, ed. Walter Müller-Seidel (Darmstadt, 1966).

Murr *Lebens-Ansichten des Katers Murr*, ed. Walter Müller-Seidel (Darmstadt, 1966). El and Murr are in the same volume.

S E.T.A. Hoffmann, *Die Serapions-Brüder*, ed. Walter Müller-Seidel (Darmstadt, 1966).

SW E.T.A. Hoffmann, *Späte Werke*, ed. Walter Müller-Seidel (Darmstadt, 1966).

1

Hoffmann, the Man and His Time

ONCE AGAIN ERNST THEODOR AMADEUS HOFFMANN'S novels and tales have become popular. Familiar with the art of
surrealism, the agonies of anti-heroes in recent fiction, and
the theater of the absurd, today's reader has gained a new
perspective on Hoffmann. Admired by many German,
French, Russian, and English authors as one of the most
original talents in German romantic literature, he was rejected by others as an artist whose work gave no hope for a
true regeneration of human nature. Today he is no longer
regarded merely as the master of horror and ghost stories
but rather as a novelist who sought to expose the apparent
irrationality and absurdity of existence, a view that is perhaps as much determined by the thinking of our age as by
Hoffmann's intentions.

No more striking figure emerges from the pages of
Hoffmann's tales than that of the author himself. Of small
stature, pale complexion, piercing eyes, hooked nose,

dressed in a brown tuxedo, he vexed many a casual visitor to Lutter's Tavern in Berlin with his appearance, mannerisms, and humor, while he enjoyed his wine with his friend, the actor Ludwig Devrient. His life was jarred by almost incredible hardships. As a child he had to endure the constant admonishments of a hysterical mother. As a young jurist he lost his position with the Prussian civil service when French troops occupied Poland. For years he tried unsuccessfully to establish himself as composer, conductor, and music critic. Finally he was appointed judge in Prussia and became widely recognized as a highly capable, uncompromising jurist, but later on his deathbed he was harassed by Berlin's corrupt police commissioner.

Hoffmann was born on January 24, 1776, in Königsberg, culturally the liveliest city in East Prussia. His parents were divorced when he was three. He was raised by a music-loving aunt and uncle after the situation in the home of his mother became too difficult. During his school years Hoffmann learned to play the organ, piano, and violin, wrote his first compositions, and formed a lasting friendship with Theodor Gottlieb Hippel. In 1792 he began to study law at the University of Königsberg. After passing his examinations in 1795, he entered the Prussian legal system in which he slowly rose from assistant magistrate to councilor and finally judge on the Supreme Court. Hoffmann was assigned positions in Glogau (1796–1798), Berlin (1798–1800), Posen (1800–1802), Plock (1802–1804), and Warsaw (1804–1807). While in Posen he married Maria Thekla Michalina Rohrer (Trzcińska), a young Polish girl. The small provincial towns offered him little stimulation, but in Berlin and Warsaw he enjoyed opera, concerts, the theater, and became acquainted with the writings of Tieck, Novalis, and Brentano. Throughout this period he continued to compose music which followed the tradition of the old masters.

On November 28, 1806, French troops invaded and occupied Warsaw. With the demise of the Prussian govern-

ment and its courts, Hoffmann suddenly found himself job-
less. Returning to Berlin, he met Chamisso, Fichte, and
Schleiermacher, but failed to secure a new position. From
Posen came word of his daughter's death and his wife's
grave illness. Finally, by advertising in a newspaper, he received an offer as composer and conductor at the theater in
Bamberg. He soon relinquished conducting but until 1812
continued both to compose for the theater and to advise its
director. Hoffmann's musical compositions include a mass,
choruses, canzonettas, a symphony, piano sonatas, a harp
quintet, the operettas *Die Maske* (1799), *Scherz, List und
Rache* (1801), *Die lustigen Musikanten* (1805), and the op-
eras *Aurora* (1811) and *Undine* (1814/15).

The publication of his first short story "Gluck" ["Ritter
Gluck"] in 1809 marked a turning point in Hoffmann's life.
He started writing critical reviews of musical compositions
and performances while giving private music lessons in
order to support himself. During that period he fell passionately in love with one of his students, Julia Mark (Marc).
The experience of unrequited love which haunted him for
many years is reflected in several of his stories.

After spending two years as conductor (1813–1814) intermittently in Leipzig and Dresden, witnessing among
other skirmishes the battle between French and Allied
troops at Dresden on August 26 and 27, 1813, Hoffmann
finally obtained a secure position as judge in Berlin. He held
the position of councilor and later judge on the Supreme
Court until his death in 1822. These were his happiest and
most successful years as jurist and artist. Publishers vied
with each other for his tales. His opera *Undine*, based on
Fouqué's tale and considered the first romantic opera, was
successfully performed in 1816. His friends included Julius
Hitzig, Ludwig Devrient, the physician Johann Ferdinand
Koreff, and the authors Chamisso, Fouqué, and Carl Wilhelm Salice-Contessa. After the Carlsbad Decrees of 1819
the Prussian government sought to crush the spirit of stu-

15

dent and youth groups who demanded both constitutional rights and complete governmental reform. Hoffmann was appointed to a commission investigating the activities of the reform movement. Honest, scrupulous, and impartial, Hoffmann refused to aid the Prussian government and released Roediger and Jahn, two of its most outspoken critics. Furthermore, he included a biting satire of the politically inspired harassment in *Master Flea* [*Meister Floh*, 1822], a tale that nevertheless clearly shows that Hoffmann was not really concerned about political democracy but was deeply troubled about life as a whole. Amidst efforts by Berlin's Police Commissioner Kamptz to have him recalled from office, Hoffmann died on June 25, 1822.

Although Hoffmann did not achieve lasting fame through his musical compositions, his literary works did inspire a host of other composers. Leading the list of ever-popular musical works based on Hoffmann's tales are Schumann's eight piano fantasies, *Kreisleriana*, Opus 16 (1838); Delibes's *Coppélia ou la fille aux yeux d'émail* (1870), based on *Der Sandmann*; Offenbach's *Tales of Hoffmann* (1881), whose most brilliant and successful performance in Germany took place under the direction of Max Reinhardt in Berlin's Grossen Schauspielhaus (1932); and Tchaikovsky's *The Nutcracker* (1891/92). Though these four compositions are performed frequently, others continue to appeal to a select audience. Among them are Tchaikovsky's opera, *The Queen of Spades* (1870), based on a Pushkin novel which was inspired by Hoffmann's "Spielerglück," Gasparo Spontini's *Olympia* (1821), Eduard Schütt's *Signor Formica* (1892), György Kósa's *Anselmus di ak* [*The Scholar Anselmus*, 1944/45], Siegmund von Hausegger's *Zinnober*, produced in Munich by Richard Strauss on June 19, 1898, and Paul Hindemith's *Cardillac* (1926). Themes and motifs introduced by Hoffmann recur in Joseph Weigl's *Die eiserne Pforte* (1823), Gian Francesco Malipiero's *I Capriccio di Callot* (1941/42), and Tibor Harsányi's *Illusion, ou l'histoire d'un miracle* (1948). Both Ture Rangström and Bernhard Sekles acknowledge their debt to Hoffmann in the titles of specific works: the former names a string quartet "Ein Nachtstück in E.T.A. Hoffmanns Manier," while the latter entitles his Opus 21, "Kleine Suite dem Andenken E.T.A. Hoffmanns."

Hoffmann's impact on the literary scene of his time, his influence on European literature, and the parallels between themes and motifs of his works and those of other writers have been well documented by now. Undoubtedly his tales called forth not only great admiration but also deep aversion. Of his contemporaries, Chamisso, Fouqué, and Heine praised him. Goethe was delighted by his creative imagination but condemned the absence of an ethical commitment. It is doubtful whether Ludwig Tieck and Jean Paul recognized Hoffmann's greatness. Certainly their noncommittal judgments show little understanding for his work. Eichendorff and Sir Walter Scott rejected him as an author whose boundless imagination knew no restraint. Perhaps the most outspoken criticism of the time against Hoffmann came from Ludwig Börne. In his review essay "Humoralpathologie" and in a review of *The Serapion Brethren* [*Die Serapions-Brüder*, 1819/21], he decried the diseased, poisoned, and hopeless world of death portrayed by Hoffmann, a world in which man is forever separated by an eternal gulf from heaven and finally plunges into an abyss of despair.[1] But the great dramatist Friedrich Hebbel who belonged to the next generation already perceived the extraordinary modernity of Hoffmann's work. He felt that *The Devil's Elixirs* [*Die Elixiere des Teufels*, 1815/16] showed a completely new perspective on the novel.

Hoffmann was received and read with great enthusiasm in France and Russia. By 1833 an edition of his works had appeared in France. Ten years later he had become the best-known German romantic. Among French authors fascinated by Hoffmann were Musset, Balzac, Sainte-Beuve,

Nerval, and Gautier. In *Curiosités esthétiques* Baudelaire noted particularly Hoffmann's peculiar sense of humor and described him as essentially a poet of the absurd. In Russia Hoffmann was considered one of the great masters of German literature next to Goethe and Heine. Widely read between 1829 and 1840, admired by Herzen, Pushkin, Dostoevsky, and Gogol, he was of all German authors "the most thoroughly known in Russia and excited the most extensive influence there." [2]

2

A New Look at Hoffmann

HOFFMANN'S WRITINGS APPEARED AT A CRITICAL moment on the European literary scene. Romantic literature was still sweeping the continent but a new pessimism was spreading among the transcendentalist philosophers. And the advent of a sober appraisal of man's existence was only a decade away. Since Hoffmann was the spiritual child of his age, his work reflects stylistically conflicting tendencies. Consequently literary critics and scholars have sometimes classified him as a typical romantic author, sometimes as a forerunner of the realistic tradition. Judgments of his work range from the view that he was an entertaining author to the conviction that he was "the greatest narrator of German romanticism" with lasting appeal.[1] Opinions still differ today though his work has been systematically reappraised during the last two decades.[2]

The fascinating combination of realistic elements and fantastic visions in Hoffmann's narrations has remained of particular interest. Despite differences in interpretation, which are to be expected, most studies agree that reality and the realm of fantasy constitute distinct levels in the fictional matrix of his works. Whereas most investigations in past decades had been preoccupied with the visionary sphere which seemed to veil the ideational significance of the works, several recent critics have pointed out that Hoffmann was a keen observer, indeed, a biting critic of society and social conditions.[3]

Nevertheless, Hoffmann's primary concern was man and not an objective, truthful picture of social conditions. Although at times he carefully describes the setting for a story or scene and succeeds in creating lively characters with vivid features and traits, such descriptions invariably serve a specific artistic function. They may characterize a figure, help create an atmosphere, or set the tone for the action.[4] Just as frequently Hoffmann resorts to clichés or presents a picture of the world which seems to consist of artificial scenery—a few trees or houses painted on a canvas and among them people, more phantom than real, tumbling about like leaves blown by a storm.[5] Though Hoffmann shared with other romantic authors a view of nature as a dynamic force that could rejuvenate man spiritually, nature often fades in his tales into an indistinct blur. What impresses the reader are cacophonous sounds, sudden movements, the projections of a character's unconscious, and real or imagined action full of excitement. It almost appears as if Hoffmann felt that man could express his anxiety and obsessions easier through preverbal action or incantations than through language.

Like many of his contemporaries, Hoffmann was devoted to high artistic ideals and upheld the ethos of art against utilitarian demands. By opening up vistas of beauty, he felt that art could free man from the shackles of the constantly shifting demands of life, enable him to find true self-expression, and ultimately increase his cultural awareness.

Still, this ethos did not inhibit Hoffmann from exploiting literary fads. In combining the beautiful with the ugly in his tales, Hoffmann followed a trend noticeable among the late romantics. Like theirs his creative imagination reached toward Olympian visions of the sublime and satanic revelations of horror, evil, and man's inner compulsions. Those studies which diagnose in his works either a dualistic view of life or three distinct spheres of reality, dream world, and absolute truth have raised important structural questions. Two principal but conflicting explanations have been offered for the juxtaposition of reality to the visionary realm. One states that Hoffmann carefully smoothes transitions and consciously seeks to obliterate them.[6] The other holds that transitions are sudden and charged with tensions.[7] Most promising, however, seem to be those investigations which either explore themes and motifs in Hoffmann's works or concentrate on his narrative technique.[8] His style has been characterized as polyphonic, culminating in a heightened intensity of conflicting and contrasting voices;[9] the structure of his stories has been compared to that of riddles which heighten the reader's suspense, and to autobiographical forms.[10]

No judgment of Hoffmann's achievement seems possible without considering the existential situation of his heroes. The most persistent view expressed by scholars rests precariously upon the tenet that Hoffmann's fictional characters yearn for a spiritual harmony which can be attained only in an ethereal realm of beauty and truth. The energy which sustains them springs from the unwavering faith in this ideal. Their mode of existence is judged as a relentless struggle in which they seek to free themselves from the wheel of life. Consequently, critics have not only underscored the inevitably dualistic world view of the protagonists in Hoffmann's narrations but have also distinguished between their momentary tragedy and their eventual salvation. This assessment has a seductive charm, because it is essentially optimistic in emphasizing the vision of a cosmic harmony which consoles man for the ordeals of life and promises to redeem him.

But does not this optimism, largely derived from interpretations of *The Golden Pot* [*Der goldne Topf*, 1814] and those fairy tales in which Hoffmann seems to resolve metaphysical contradictions in a myth of transcendence, overlook the profound pessimism pervading most of his works? Do not his transcendental speculations indicate also a disturbing awareness of man's ontological insecurity? Is it not true that Hoffmann's heroes are destined to live in a threatening world even though they may dimly perceive or even experience in a clairvoyant moment a universal harmony? A pessimistic spirit, for instance, is the dominant element in Hoffmann's characterization of the heroes in three major narratives: *The Devil's Elixirs, Life and Opinions of Tomcat Murr* [*Lebens-Ansichten des Katers Murr*, 1820/21], and *Master Flea*. Flung into a capricious, often malevolent world, threatened by a sinister fate, and caught in a web of their own fantasies, the heroes seek to master their destinies and struggle to assert themselves, no matter how brutal or pathetic life may be.

The reader who looks for a sublimation of life in Hoffmann's works will instead frequently find the exposition of evil, an affinity for death and self-destruction, the projection of semi-consciousness, primitive emotions, and the tyranny of fear and anxiety. Not surprisingly, scholars who recognized that the literature of romanticism tended not only toward transcendental speculation but also toward pessimism, nihilism, and a "myth of evil" have always pointed to Bonaventura, Jean Paul, and Hoffmann as authors who succeeded best in capturing the spirit of negation and evil.[11] The cipher of an inexplicable fate was interpreted as the expression of man's inability to master forces in life which were apparently beyond his control, and alter ego projections were regarded as the first indication of the modern crisis in man's identity. Yet, as long as the view persists that two distinct spheres, reality and a transcendental realm, clash in Hoffmann's writings, the basic structure and the intent of his work will be misunderstood.

Indeed, the contrast between sublime vision and primeval fear, reinforced by the themes of self-transcendence and self-realization, forms an essential part of a grand design. Against the background of an apparently stable bourgeois society Hoffmann paints a picture of man trapped in a cage from which he tries in vain to break out. Primitive instincts that previously seemed tamed suddenly overwhelm individuals, and demonic, unexplainable forces seem to rule the lives of persons who are caught in a deep identity crisis. Included in the design are metaphors which seem to rise straight out of the darkness of the unconscious alter ego projections, such as the motif of drinking blood, pictures of incest, murder, and human sacrifice, and the preference for masks noticeable in the frozen eerie smile of many characters.

Admittedly, it is more rewarding for the humanistic scholar to point to revelations of beauty and goodness than to those of ugliness and evil. Yet, to do justice to Hoffmann's works one must observe the prevailing ideological and structural tension between self-transcendence in a sublime vision of cosmic consciousness and self-realization in a harsh, adverse world. In discussing the themes and motifs of Hoffmann's grand design, the present study focuses on the basic clash between the yearning for innocence and the intense fascination with evil and destruction. Central to my argument is the view that the grand design of man's existential plight structurally unifies Hoffmann's writings. Its basic features include vistas of beauty and of nature animated by friendly spirits together with visions of horror and a demonic world. It reveals a part of man's nature which we

prefer to overlook: the ruthless assertion of the will, the desire to inflict pain, and the lust for destruction. With his design of the tortured self Hoffmann broke with the conventions of his day and anticipated a major concern of modern
existential literature.

Self-realization and
Self-transcendence

THE THEME OF SELF-REALIZATION APPEARS in Hoff-mann's first story "Gluck." The narrative concentrates on the experiences of an apparently mentally disturbed but gifted composer who imagines that he is Gluck. Tormented because the society in which he lives does not share his high ideal of music and because he himself seems incapable of attaining his vision of a cosmic harmony, he is driven by his demon to compose and, reaching for an elusive goal, yearns for inspiration. According to his testimony, he suffers years of agony, dreaming and hoping, and fighting the temptation to drift into a dream world, before he finally experiences a complete union with nature and God. Hoffmann conveys Gluck's emotions during this transcendence through a brilliant poetic picture: a sunflower opens and a radiant eye (inspiration, grace) within its calyx awakens Gluck's creative powers; now music emanates from him which in turn inspires nature; suddenly flames encircle him, the eye disappears and he is in the calyx (FN, 19). After his overwhelming vision, in which he ascends to the eternal source of life, he is flung back to earth and, as the blank musical score shows, fails to cast his experience into artistic form. While this progression of Gluck's experiences does not present major problems in interpretation, his breakthrough does. The observation that he liberated himself from society and perceived ultimate truth is not adequate, because it ignores Gluck's fate.[1] After his vision, which echoes a profoundly religious experience, the protagonist of Hoffmann's story is condemned to live in despair, rendered powerless since he is incapable of recreating in music the emotions he experienced. His tragedy is twofold. He transcended himself but lost his identity because he pressed beyond all limits of perception and is now forced to live in a world which does not understand him: "Then I was condemned to walk among the uninspired philistines like a departed spirit—formless, so that no one would recognize me, until the sunflower will lift me up again to the eternal" (FN, 23). Furthermore he is doomed as an artist, for he fails to cast his visions into form. Consequently he completely assumes the identity of the composer Gluck in whose works he divines a kindred perception. Hoffmann's narrative, then, probes into the failure of self-realization which stretches the protagonist's inner tensions beyond endurance.

A variation of the theme occurs in a central section in "Don Juan" (1813). In Hoffmann's interpretation, Mozart's hero becomes the prototype of fallen man who is driven to destruction because his infinite longing cannot come to terms with existence. Endowed with innate nobility, talented and spirited, he is touched by a divine spark (FN, 75). Incapable of a genuinely religious experience of God's existence, however, he seeks fulfillment of his yearning for an absolute not beyond but within life. Dissatisfied with the frenzied activity which has become the true basis of his life and forever disappointed by his amours, he finally comes to despise mankind and proclaims himself the master of the fate of others. Now his autonomy defies the onslaught of spiritual thoughts; indeed it negates the idea of a creator: "Every seduction of a beloved bride, every happiness of the lovers, destroyed by a sudden misfortune, is a beautiful triumph over that antagonistic power, a triumph which exalts him ever more above confining life, above nature, indeed above the creator! He really desires to leave life but only to plunge into Orcus" (FN, 76). It is Hoffmann's judgment, then, that Don Juan is already condemned to tragic loneliness while he seems to revel in pleasure and that his negation of faith in favor of a new belief in man's absolute autonomy leads to self-annihilation.

Hoffmann's characterization of artists, ranging from a series of vignettes in "Kreisleriana" (1810/14) to the portrait of Johannes Kreisler in *Tomcat Murr* and from "Jaques Callot" (1814) to "The Cousin's Corner Window" ["Des Vetters Eckfenster," 1822], embodies many aspects which contribute to a pronounced tragic dimension. The individual pictures of musicians, poets, and painters differ from story to story. Several essential characteristics in the artistic disposition, however, such as the artist's view of nature, his stance toward the world, and his temperament recur throughout Hoffmann's works.[2] And while the emerging composite picture can hardly be identified as a myth of the artist, its elements reveal the contours of a deeply troubled and quite modern artist type.

This artist, who has an almost prophetic faith in art's ability to heal man, has retained a childlike belief in his visions of an enchanted world,[3] and is willing to sacrifice "happiness, wordly fortunes, indeed his life" (FN, 98) for his art. But Anselmus, Berthold, Berklinger, and Kreisler are forced to live in a society in which true art has become an anachronism. Kreisler soon learns that the general public can no longer comprehend the mystery, beauty, and significance of music but only listens to it in order to be diverted and entertained.[4] And Anselmus finds his paradise only in the never-never land of Atlantis where the charm of poesy is all-pervasive. The realities of the world of bureaucrats and courtiers leave no room for his imaginative transformation of life. Thus when Lindhorst relates his family history, Anselmus perceives in it a poetic myth while the other listeners burst into loud laughter at the "Oriental fabrication." Life, "all the mad activities of a world inhabited by puppets" (Murr, 358), seems to approximate the complex yet predetermined motions of an intricate mechanism. The court of Prince Irenäus with its predictable behavior and ceremonial movements resembles the toy castle in *Nutcracker and the King of Mice* [*Nussknacker und Mausekönig*, 1816]. Indeed, everyone's actions appear to be predetermined. The artist sees it as his mission to save man from such a machinelike existence and self-imposed limitations by stirring in him "a sensibility for the ultimate, divine power" and to help him rediscover the dreams of his childhood, his dignity, and his humanity. The struggle and suffering of Anselmus and Kreisler clearly show the many difficulties besetting the artist as reformer and healer of man. The artist is horrified by a world in which men have been reduced to being technicians and holds up to society the vision of a new man. Yet few understand his aims or react favorably to his demands.[5] No wonder he is tempted either to make peace with society and forego his ideal or to reject its values and embrace his dreams.

Hoffmann already hints at this conflict in *The Golden Pot*, in which he skillfully expands the familiar fairy-tale motif of the simpleton who, because he has a good heart, triumphs over all adverse circumstances and is rewarded in the end. The hero of the fairy tale, the student Anselmus, is introduced as a young man beset by misfortune. He ardently desires to be like others; indeed, his fondest dream is to become one day a Privy Councilor. But an inexorable and inexplicable demon trips him whenever he seems close to success (FN, 180–82). As the plot unfolds the reader begins to wonder whether the childlike, poetic disposition of Anselmus, which sets him apart from his friends, is really responsible for his troubles. For, in contrast to the philistines around him who regard inspiration as intoxication, as a disease to be cured, he becomes enchanted by the sounds of nature and searches in the whispering trees for the true meaning of life. Nature, in which Anselmus gropes for a harmony lost to man, responds to his yearning. Serpentina, a golden green snake, beckons him and awakens his love. She inspires him during his apprenticeship when he progresses in writing from the first steps to mastery; she guides him in deciphering the true significance of the myth of creation, and finally helps him mature into a true poet (FN, 251) who understands the voices of nature. But before Anselmus realizes that Serpentina symbolizes poetic inspiration—"Is the bliss of Anselmus anything else but a life in poetry, a poetry to which the sacred harmony of all beings is revealed as the deepest secret of nature?"—in which he must firmly believe, he is overcome by doubts and by the desire to forego the difficult poetic calling for the pleasures of bourgeois life. The ensuing action revolves around the conflict between the dedication to poetry and the acceptance of a mundane existence, between the Promethean spark and sensuous desires. The final outcome is by no means assured. Anselmus is tempted by Veronika, a beautiful girl who loves him and holds the promise of becoming a good wife. Her materialistic aspirations, however, contrast sharply with Anselmus's idealism. Veronika's flights of fancy are limited to wishful dreams in which she sees herself as the wife of the court councilor Anselmus, giving orders to her cook while sitting at the breakfast table near a window where she can be admired by passing young gentlemen (FN, 204). Bewitched by her charm, Anselmus at one point considers becoming a "useful citizen"—that is, a court councilor—in order to marry her. But since his view of the world cannot really be reconciled with Veronika's, he would have to betray his ideals if she became his wife.

As soon as Anselmus momentarily doubts his ideal and briefly confuses his ethereal vision with earthly love, his inspiration leaves him. Nature loses her charmed appearance: flowers seem drab; birds whose song had enchanted him begin to screech; the magic symbols of poetry remain meaningless; and above all he can no longer write (FN, 238–39). Hoffmann conveys the loss of inspiration and the subsequent suffering and recognition of human limitation through the image of Anselmus trapped in the bottle. Caged, unable to move, he suffers the agony of a man who is brutally crushed by immovable weights (FN, 240). Noticing other prisoners, Anselmus laments their bitter fate. They, however, burst into loud laughter. Seen from their perspective they are completely free: "The student is mad, he imagines he is sitting in a glass bottle but is standing on the Elbe Bridge, looking straight down into the water. Let's go!" (FN, 241). Inspiration returns to Anselmus only after he renounces all further doubts and every aspiration to live in the world as an ordinary citizen. Then his deep yearning is answered. Anselmus transcends himself, an act accompanied by a symphony of colors, scents, and sounds:

The trees and the bushes whisper louder—the brooks rejoice clearer and happier—birds and colorful insects dance in the vapor—a gay, joyful, jubilant tumult in the air, the water, and on the earth celebrates the festival of love! . . . Now Anselmus raises his head as if encircled with a bright halo.—Is it the glance, the words, the melody?—You can hear it: "Serpentina! Faith in you, love for you has revealed to me the innermost spirit of nature!" [FN, 254]

The clash between two opposite modes of existence motivates the action in the fairy tale and contributes greatly to two dominant artistic patterns: one of detail and concrete universal, the other of energy and harmony. The narrative opens with an exact description of day, time, and setting.

The hero, his frustrations, and his attempts to escape from the restrictions of society are brought into sharp focus. Hoffmann enhances and interweaves these details with the fairy-tale motif of the innocent simpleton. Whereas the fantasies and poetic visions of Anselmus characterize him as a romantic dreamer, they also reveal the universal significance of his person and adventures. He is an artist whose vision of man's harmonious existence in the universe transcends the views of his time. Conversely, the precise characterization of bourgeois life, of Veronika's dreams and environment, and of the trapped Anselmus point to the imagery of the cage, of man imprisoned in life by narrow interests and desires. In addition, the symbolic struggle between Lindhorst and the forces of evil illuminates the incompatibility of the vision of a new basis for man's existence with passive acquiescence in the existing order.

The tension resulting from the metaphysical conflict is reinforced by a technique of dynamic movement which stresses contrasts, unexpected juxtapositions, and surprising events. Anselmus and the other characters rush from scene to scene. The tale's twelve vigils form a pattern which not only interrupts the temporal sequence by intermingling future with past or present events but also enables the author to account for apparently inexplicable incidents in later vigils. Yet explanations create new mysteries and increase the suspense which is finally resolved in the vista of man in harmony with himself and nature. At this moment the surge of energy is released in the picture of nature celebrating the joy of life.

Humor, a gentle irony, and the affirmation of beauty generally prevail in *The Golden Pot*. Though satirized, the world of the philistines is accepted as part of life. Even Veronika's dreams come true. She marries a councilor and should be able to live as she has envisioned. Still, even the enchanted, poetic world of Atlantis cannot hide the unresolved existential dilemma of the narrative. The spiral, upward thrust of the fairy tale, coupled with the imagery of isolation, reveals that the poet's vision remains a postulate. He has yet to find a new basis for man's existence in society.

The threatening undercurrents of the fairy tale become more noticeable, however, in the light of other stories. The feeling of total helplessness and despair which overcomes Anselmus after he assumes that his ideal actually exists in Veronika is shared by the painters Traugott and Berthold. They too see in the beautiful, saintly women they encounter the incarnation of their ideals.[6] Traugott, the young merchant in "The Artus Exchange" ["Der Artushof," 1817] who longs to become an artist, is inspired by an inner vision of his ideal. He almost despairs of the task of giving his experience a distinct form: "He perceives the ideal and yet feels helpless to reach it; he believes that it has escaped irretrievably. But then Olympian courage rises in him, he struggles and fights. Despair is transformed into a gentle longing which strengthens him and spurs him on to reach for the beloved who seems closer and closer and yet remains distant forever" (S, 153). Upon seeing a portrait of Felizitas, the daughter of the insane painter Berklinger, he is suddenly overwhelmed by the recognition that she embodies his ideal (S, 158). Seized by passion he searches for the girl but realizes finally that she must remain unattainable if he is to become a productive artist: "You are creative art alive in me" (S, 169).

For Berthold in "The Jesuit Church in G." ["Die Jesuiterkirche in G.," 1816] the confusion of the pure ideal with life leads to complete disaster. Endowed like Anselmus with an innocent artistic disposition, Berthold ceaselessly struggles for artistic perfection in order to capture in his paintings the vision of supreme beauty which haunts him. He tries to express his idea first in portraits, later in landscapes, but fails because he only succeeds in imitating reality perfectly without ever conveying the eternal, typical form. In desperation he succumbs to his dreams:

I was joyous and blissful only in sweet dreams. . . . Enveloped by magic waves of scent I was resting in green bushes and nature's voice murmured melodiously through the dark forest.— Listen—listen carefully, sacred initiate! Hear the primeval sounds of creation which assume forms that you can perceive. And as I heard the chords more distinctly, it seemed as if a new sense had arisen in me which comprehended with marvelous lucidity everything that had remained a secret. As if in exotic hieroglyphics I sketched the revealed secret with flames into the air. [FN, 430]

But the secret is revealed only in his dreams. He remains incapable of expressing the infinite idea in a finite form and despairs.

All his difficulties vanish when he beholds in a grotto near Naples a woman from whose countenance his vision seems to radiate. Inspired, he can now express his ideal in paintings. Later, during the revolution he comes upon a mob scene, where a beautiful girl, Princess Angiola, is about to be murdered, and he is suddenly overwhelmed by the realization that he had seen her at the grotto, that she had been no apparition but actually existed. He hurls himself upon the assassin and saves her. His destruction and demise as an artist are brought about by his subsequent passionate love for Angiola who returns his feelings. When she models for a projected painting through which he hopes to establish himself as a great master, he finds himself unable to breathe life into it. Once again he is overcome by despair. But he realizes only much later, after he has deserted both her and his son, that he foundered on the incongruity between ideal and reality: "If one strives for the highest . . . the ultimate of divine nature, the Promethean spark in man . . . one stands on a narrow ledge, the abyss is open and the courageous venturer soars above. Then a satanic deception shows him below, down there what he yearned to see above the stars" (FN, 419).

An allusion to this threat to the artist's creativity can also be found in Chrysostomus's narration ("Johannes

Kreisler's Certificate" ["Johannes Kreislers Lehrbrief," 1816]) of the bard who loves a beautiful young girl and nightly sings with her strange, magic chants. One morning he disappears—leaving behind his broken lyre and the girl whom he has stabbed to death (FN, 322–23). These pure, feminine figures, then, present both a source of artistic inspiration and a menace. The artist who remains at a distance and contemplates feminine beauty as a form through which he can express his ideal can achieve a breakthrough in his production. Characteristically it is an innocent, almost pious love "that is not restricted in time or space, that is eternal like the spirit of the world," which enables the artist to cast his vision into lasting form (Murr, 431). The artist who is overpowered by his passion, however, destroys the divine light of his ideal.[7] He awakens one day and realizes that the beautiful girl is in reality a strange, seductive temptress who possesses his body and soul. He revolts but his vision together with his spiritual essence are lost.

The symbolism of the virgin and the vampire constitutes one of the most elaborate forms of doubling in Hoffmann's works. It occurs in many stories. Sometimes the women are easily identified because the hero or narrator of the story is confronted by a clear choice between a pure, good woman and a vampire, as for instance in "The Story of the Lost Reflection" ["Die Geschichte vom verlornen Spiegelbilde," 1815] and "The Sandman" ["Der Sandmann," 1815]. In *Tomcat Murr* the characteristics of the women remain veiled until they engage in an almost dramatic struggle for Kreisler's affection. Virgin and vampire are fused into a single person in "The Artus Exchange" and "The Jesuit Church in G." Could it be that the struggle between artist and temptress reflects Hoffmann's personal tragedy with Julia Mark?[8] The symbols, however, belong to an established tradition. The choice of the untouched woman has religious overtones in recalling the cult of the Virgin Mary, while the vampires are reminiscent of Lilith and the Whore of Babylon. In Hoffmann's tales the symbolism of the virgin and the vampire reflects the struggle between ideal and reality, between the angelic and satanic vision in man. The artist figures are especially vulnerable since their search for the ideal demands a total commitment.

The artists in Hoffmann's works experience moments in which they celebrate a cult of nature as the fountain of universal harmony, a feeling perhaps best captured by the atmosphere in the poet's paradise, Atlantis. Hoffmann, as his letters indicate, was able to feel a similar bliss: "As I sat this evening in the beautiful, awe-inspiring path among the trees, as the fragrance of the blooming jasmine, scotch thistles, lilies, and roses enveloped me, I felt an indescribable pleasure arising within me like glorious divine music . . . the world spirit himself played the invisible strings of the universe, resounding in every heart and awakening the inner voices so that they could join in the chords of nature!" [9] The idolization of nature seems to spring from the belief that the contemplation of her forms which exist of inner necessity will impart to man the vision of a desirable existence, in which thought and emotion are in dynamic balance.[10] But Hoffmann's reflections also indicate his awareness that such a view is fraught with dangers both for the artist still searching for a form of expression and for the one experiencing a crisis in his production. Thus Berthold succumbs temporarily to a purely passive, nebulous longing and, unable or unwilling to observe reality, experiences nature subjectively. Kreisler briefly abandons all work and rages against himself and others, because he cannot express his vision. And Berklinger becomes insane when he fails to cast his idea into form.

While Hoffmann usually depicts artists as deeply troubled and suffering persons, he was, as "Signor Formica" (1819) shows, capable of a more lighthearted view. Many observations scattered throughout his works indicate that he had a definite and positive conception of a true, creative artist. He stressed that ideally the artist's temperament should combine the capacity of visionary perception, a dedication to ideals, and the ability to observe the world objectively. To be sure, he himself had a tendency to refer frequently to the pleasurable experiences of the semiconscious state between waking and sleeping as well as to those of the roving fantasy.[11] In a "visionary state" the artist even seems capable of perceiving intuitively the total idea or structure of a projected work.[12] However, since the vision not only expands the mind but of necessity leads to a dematerialization of reality, artists, especially poets and painters, should retain a firm bond with the world. Indeed, a careful observation of nature almost seems to be a prerequisite for artistic creation. Still, the artist can never be satisfied with a simple imitation of nature's varied forms.[13] His perception, Hoffmann argues, should become a conscious process in which he observes characteristic aspects, comprehends the true significance of what he has seen, and begins to analyze the object, scene, or material for their artistic possibilities. "The true poet penetrates human nature to its innermost depth, he masters appearance because his mind captures prismatically the thousand reflections of life and then reflects them." [14]

Equally important for the inspired artist is the ability to reflect critically upon his experience and to distance himself from his work in order to look at it objectively.[15] In the discussion of *The Serapion Brethren* Lother extends this view to the author of romantic fairy tales: "I would assure you . . . that the poor author would gain little if fantastic ideas were to arise within him, as in a bewildering dream; such visions are utterly useless unless carefully considered, judged, and ordered by a clear mind before a lovely but strong thread is spun out of them. Moreover, I would say that a serene disposition is necessary for the creation of a work that appears to be arbitrary and formless. Especially such a work must have a stable core." [16] In line with this reasoning

Hoffmann refers to the strong consciousness which is insep-
arable from true genius.[17]

Thus the artist's creativity is threatened not only by the
inability of society to understand his aims but also by his
own failure to give his visions lasting form. Gluck's blank
notepaper (FN, 23) and Berklinger's empty canvas (S, 156)
reveal this problem. Berklinger like Gluck is a deeply tragic
figure. His early paintings had equaled Van Dyck's masterpieces. A vision of ultimate beauty in the form of a regained
paradise overwhelms him and strains his imagination and
creative power beyond their limits. In the actual world he
cannot find forms corresponding to the symphony of colors,
scents, and sounds that he experiences (S, 157). Ultimately,
Berklinger demands that his art transcend itself and become
reality: "My painting is not supposed to *signify,* it *is*" (FN,
156) or, as Archibald MacLeish said of poetry, "A poem
should not mean, but be." In Berklinger's view the work of
art is no longer an expression of a specific experience but of
infinite yearning which he cannot express in concrete forms
and figures. As a result of the struggle he becomes insane.
He and Gluck actually attempt to go beyond abstract art.
Both are shattered by the incommensurable task of trying to
express infinity. Hoffmann apparently assumed at one time
that a musical genius might solve the problem in a sym-
phonic composition: "Music [instrumental music] opens up
to man an unknown realm in which nothing corresponds to
our world, a realm in which he surrenders to the inexpres-
sible and leaves all those emotions behind which can be
identified . . . even experiences that have their origin in life
transport us into an eternal realm" (W, 13: 41). But Kreisler,
and also Dürer in "The Enemy" ["Der Feind," 1822], as
well as the cousin in "The Cousin's Corner Window" recognize that every artist must find a form through which he can
speak to his audience.[18]

4

Struggle for a New Vision or the Infernal Circle

IN THE FIGURE OF JOHANNES KREISLER, Hoffmann has created his most memorable artist hero and certainly one of the most problematic characters in German romantic literature. Though everything Hoffmann wrote about him has remained fragmentary, he succeeded in bringing a dynamic personality to life. The inconclusive nature of the partial account appears to be an excellent artistic device reflecting Kreisler's struggles with problems which elude permanent solution. Hoffmann traced the musician's life to some extent in *Life and Opinions of Tomcat Murr* by showing his coming of age, his earliest impressions, his decision to become a civil servant, and the compulsion to compose which drives him into the world. To the reader of "Kreisleriana" and to Kreisler's fictitious contemporaries who inform us of his life, he seems like a prophet who suddenly appears from an unknown region, lives and suffers among others in the world, and, leaving his message, disappears again (FN, 25–26, 284).

Similar to the modern artist types of Joyce, Benn, Thomas Mann, and Valéry, he experiences the difficulties of the creative process as well as the conflict between the creative personality and society. He yearns to be accepted and understood by others, yet knows that life is a curse unless the world is changed by his vision of a new man whose potential has been fully developed by the appreciation of art.

Since very few people live up to the ideal projected by art, he begins to brood, then castigates and satirizes his audiences—all those good people who love to disrupt music at the most beautiful moments when "the golden sounds slowly reveal paradise" (FN, 287). Repeatedly disappointed, Kreisler delights in startling the uninspired with eccentric musical metaphors, alternately charms and repels people, and is restlessly driven from place to place.[1] He withdraws from society, spins himself into a "cocoon of music" (FN, 289), hopes to find peace at the court of Prince Irenäus, and briefly seeks refuge in a monastery (Murr, 536 ff.). But Kreisler knows that all his attempts to escape are doomed, knows that he is destined by fate to wander among those who misunderstood him: "They have handed me a wonderful crown, but the diamonds that sparkle and glisten are thousands of tears which I have shed, and the gold reflects the flames which consumed me" (FN, 294).

Burdened by his crown of tears, living in a world which Hoffmann characterizes by symbols of confinement, such as narrow rooms, listeners crowding him at the piano, and distorted landscapes around him, Kreisler begins to fear for his sanity, suddenly bursts into unmotivated gaiety, and at one point even doubts his strength to endure: "I was so depressed by the pressure of all the miserable, wretched trifles which, like poisonous insects, haunt and sting man, especially the artist in his pitiful life who would often prefer a violent end which would terminate all that eternal, pricking pain on earth" (FN, 33).[2] Yet, in the face of all the misunderstanding and even hostility, the spirit of true love and the vision of an ideal relationship between art and man never leave him.

The strong tensions in Kreisler's personality, mirrored in his bizarre behavior and the apparently unmotivated alternation of moods, reflect internal contradictions not caused solely by the conflict with society. They are rooted in his search for self-expression. Irrational impulses make it difficult for him to sustain his dedication to a high ideal. He becomes disenchanted, seeks to escape, and longs to gratify his desires. There is even a hint of the violence that characterizes the monk Medardus in his outbursts:

> Then I was seized by that indescribable restlessness which has so frequently torn me apart since my early youth. It is not the yearning . . . which originates in a higher realm and lasts eternally because it can never be fulfilled . . . no—what erupts in me is a mad, ugly desire for something that I seek restlessly in the world which, however, is hidden within me, a confused puzzling dream of a paradise of ultimate pleasure, a satisfaction so great that even the dream cannot express it but only hint at it. This feeling tortures me with the pains of Tantalus. [Murr, 355–56]

An even more significant factor seems to be the threat to Kreisler's productivity. He tends to lose himself in the onrush of his musical fantasies. Playing and composing simultaneously, he momentarily envisions the entire composition. Yet, when he is overwhelmed either by his inspiration or by the experience of beauty, he suddenly awakens and plunges back to earth, unable to sustain the creative effort. Similarly he hears as melodies the sounds of nature, rustling leaves, murmuring brooks, the wind and rain which he could transform into compositions but instead frequently fails to retain his experience in musical notes.

In effect, while Kreisler understands nature's secrets and comes closer than any other of Hoffmann's artist figures to comprehend his visions, he often seems unable or unwilling to compose consciously.[3] His advice in the "Certificate" accentuates this difficulty. He stresses that a good composer should always consciously reflect upon the "melodies and harmonies" that surround him in life. Indeed the art of composing consists of the ability to retain experiences and cast them into lasting form (FN, 326). Kreisler also has had the tragic experience of mistakenly assuming that his ideal was embodied in a young girl. Deeply wounded he suffers in agony and rages like Berthold against nature's deception (FN, 291). But unlike Berthold he refuses to surrender to his pain; instead he either ridicules the world, projects his ideal into a loftier realm, or, stimulated by a champagne punch, climbs into a bubble and thereby escapes the dreary task of writing notes.

Viewed in the light of the parallel action in *Tomcat Murr*,[4] which satirizes Murr's "creative process" and literary output, it becomes evident that Hoffmann portrays in Kreisler's struggle one aspect of the artist's general situation in a period of changing style. The tomcat's coming of age as an artist, a sequence in which Hoffmann parodies the traditional stages of the novel of development, deserves special attention since it clearly shows a potential threat to the artist's creativity by tracing the rise of the pseudo-artist who is no longer creative but blithely deceives a gullible public. Murr, an egotist of astounding proportions, is motivated from early youth to maturity by the will to excel. Aroused by an insatiable desire to copy his master and acquire knowledge, he rejects his role as tomcat, begins to read voraciously, and soon progresses from Knigge to the classics of world literature, philosophy, and scientific thought. It is of minor consequence that he never gains any real understanding, for he soon is no longer satisfied with reading. He feels the irrepressible wish to write in order to "preserve his wisdom for posterity" (Murr, 323–24). His first attempts, which he praises for their "depth and intellectual profundity," indicate that he has adopted and mastered the generally accepted aesthetic norms. He knows art must relax, entertain, and divert. Like Milo, the educated ape ("News of an Educated Young Man" ["Nachricht von einem gebildeten jungen Mann," 1814]), he arrives at a principle of artistic creation which guarantees success: once a great work has been conceived and executed by a genius, the "wise" imitator copies its idea. He then points to his work and proves that it is superior to its model (FN, 300). Murr also realizes that the whims of society's taste may dictate form and content of his work and soon learns how to impress others with knowledgeable conversation. Shocked by his skill, a professor of aesthetics begins to fear for his career and immediately sees Murr as a hated competitor. The reader may even wonder whether he is the same professor who initiated Milo into the secrets of aesthetic appreciation and intelligent conversation: that is, how to talk about feeling and coldness and the tendencies of the age, to remember a few platitudes and quotations, and above all to cultivate an infallible judgment. "The whole secret is to speak fluently, skillfully, and with ease. You will be surprised how thoughts flow to you while you speak, how wise you will suddenly be as divine rhetoric guides you to penetrate to the very source of all science and art. You might even think you are walking in labyrinths. Often you will not understand what you are saying. But then you are truly inspired" (FN, 301). It is not surprising that both Milo and Murr who completely conform to the conventions of society become popular and successful.

During his "apprenticeship years" Murr not only develops into an urbane poet, knowledgeable in all of society's follies, he also undergoes the same basic experiences of love and death as Kreisler. But whereas Kreisler's love is sublimated into a love for mankind, Murr marries, becomes a fat cat, and is divorced after being burdened with and annoyed by the trivialities of married life. The different reactions of Kreisler and Murr to death are even more telling. Kreisler suffers deeply before he realizes that man cannot escape his lot, a recognition which actually enhances his understanding of life. Murr remains basically untouched when he reflects upon the transitory nature of life. After an initial exaggerated show of emotion, he analyzes the sentimental funeral oration and then returns with the other mourners to the order of the day: eating, drinking, dancing, and making love (Murr, 574–84). The poem in which Murr expresses his emotions shows in all its ornamental splendor and triviality that he has become a facile poet who has learned nothing from life and is as intoxicated by his importance as ever (Murr, 597–99). His attitude toward the truly gifted individual also remains unchanged and is essentially the same as Milo's: "Infallible indications of the most highly cultivated genius are: a complete scorn for every effort of others; the conviction necessary to disregard completely all those who prefer to remain silent and create unassumingly; and the greatest satisfaction with one's own productions which are created without effort . . ." (FN, 304). The ease with which Murr writes cannot disguise his inability to rise above his models. He is doomed to play with and plagiarize traditional forms. His first didactic sentimental novel *Thought and Awareness or Cat and Dog*, his "immortal" philosophical work *Concerning Mousetraps and Their Influence on Temperament and Energy of Cathood*, his sonnet "Yearning for a Higher Realm" are all timely, popular copies. His fantastic skill merely accentuates the trivial meaning of his poems.[5]

That Hoffmann also parodies existing forms through Murr's plagiarisms indicates his deep awareness of the dilemma that confronts the artist who has lost faith in traditional forms and themes. Apparently Hoffmann remained dissatisfied with the experiment. His hero Kreisler rejects all parodies as barren and nihilistic, though he is completely familiar with the musical heritage and masters the traditional compositions. At the same time he is so conscious of the change or even disintegration of the old value system and the attending stylistic transition that he initially judges the harmony and symmetry of past music as inappropriate for him. His early compositions and the spontaneous preludes played by him suggest a transformation of musical forms. He seems to experiment with magical incantations but also develops a propensity to verbalize music as "Kreisler's Musical Poetic Club" ["Kreislers musikalisch-poetischer Klub," 1815] demonstrates (FN, 26, 30, 35, 290–97). Apparently he finds these experiments ineffective, for he destroys them. His basic, insurmountable dilemma is that he must find a form which can contain his chaotic visions (Murr, 310, 315) but which will also express his mystic view of a harmonious relationship between man, nature, and universe.[6]

Not surprisingly he thirsts for release, yearns to unleash his creative power: "The wonderful spirit of beautiful sounds that resides in this little mysterious instrument also lives in my soul but hidden in a cocoon it cannot move" (Murr, 342). "Johannes Kreisler's Certificate" reveals perhaps most accurately his search for expression and the only possible solution. Kreisler cannot revert to purely expressive, emotional incantations because he senses that such a reversion would open the gates to a demonic, barbaric world (FN, 322–23). Glimpses of this world which hides man's most primitive instincts seem to prompt his occasional haunting fear of insanity. "Look, he reaches with his blazing talons for my heart! . . . Do you see him lurk there, the pale ghost with his sparkling red eyes, shaking the crown of straw on his polished, bald head—and stretching his bony claws out of his torn coat toward you?" [7] But since his vision of music as a great healing power is essentially humanistic and religious, he overcomes his fear and returns to the old masters for guidance.[8] Indeed, the compositions that he does not destroy and to which he attributes lasting value reflect the spirit of a regained harmony (Murr, 537–38). Still, it would be difficult indeed to state unequivocally that Kreisler's quest ceases at this point. Since the fragment ends in the first chapter where it began, Master Abraham's admonition to Kreisler to "purify the raging inferno in his soul to a pure, bright flame," implies that the struggle continues (Murr, 310). Kreisler, punning on his name, reveals that he is torn by external and internal conflicts and finds that he is unable to break out of life's confinement: "Circles . . . in which our whole existence moves, from which we cannot break out, no matter what we do. Kreisler circles in these circles; it may happen that he pits himself against the mysterious, impenetrable power that flung him into these circles; and, tired by the leaps of the St. Vitus's dance which he is forced to dance, he yearns for liberation" (Murr, 352). This tragic picture of Kreisler caught in a web overshadows his positive view of art and his essentially humanistic attitude toward man.

Since the circle as an image of constriction recurs in the novel, Hoffmann must have concluded that Kreisler, like the other artists, cannot find true fulfillment in the world. He passionately yearns for a breakthrough in his compositions but the obstacles from within and without him seem insurmountable. While Hoffmann tends to stress the idealism and positive goal of the artist and in aesthetic discussions ("Jaques Callot," *The Serapion Brethren,* "The Cousin's Corner Window") sets forth the basic traits of a creative personality, his artist figures are either vainly struggling to speak to man or no longer creative. The final picture is one of deep gloom. The artist and society can no longer communicate. The true artist has visions either of escape and insanity or of conformity and damnation. Only performers, puppets, the Milos, and the Murrs are admired, praised, successful, and content.

5

Lebensangst and Failure

HOFFMANN PROBES INTO SIMILAR QUESTIONS RELATING
to the nature of the artist and art in "The Sandman" and
"Councilor Krespel" ["Rat Krespel," 1817]. Essentially,
however, both stories portray painful human tragedies. The
most common critical judgment on "The Sandman" discerns
the essence of the story in the hero's sustained fear of losing
his eyes, a fear which finally leads to his insanity and death.[1]
The tale's prevailing structural pattern is one of ever-in-
creasing momentum toward catastrophe. As in other stories,
Hoffmann freely employs verbs of action, sudden changes of
scenes, violent confrontations, and exaggerated contrasts.
The dominant themes, captured in the imagery of the eye,
the cage, the shattered self, and the puppet, are *Lebensangst* and the failure to realize the self in the world. The
protagonist, the student Nathanael, finds himself trapped in
the confining circle of his imagination which so dominates
his thinking that he can no longer perceive the world ration-

ally. His suffering and the final plunge from a tower seem to represent the terror of all those haunted by the eyes of a society with which they can no longer communicate.

An analysis of the action shows that the ultimate disaster is precipitated by the hero's increasing inability to distinguish between his visions of fear and actual events. There are three major stages in the action: first, Nathanael's childhood experiences which culminate in the violent death of his father; second, his love for his childhood friend Clara which leads to a tragic climax; and finally, his encounter with an Italian vendor of barometers, telescopes, and glasses, as a result of which he can no longer distinguish between illusion and reality, falls in love with Olimpia, a puppet, and sinks into insanity. The story also encompasses Nathanael's and Clara's opposing views of the events.

The three stages in the story's development correspond to the progressive deterioration of Nathanael's relationship with the world. His childhood experiences constitute the first phase of an inner struggle between the demand to grow up and a fear of life. Nathanael feels that his life has been threatened since childhood by evil, demonic powers that seek to destroy him. He associates his mother's admonition, "the sandman is coming," with the heavy steps of a mysterious stranger who visits his father. His imagination is further inflamed by a maid's tale that the sandman plucks children's eyes in order to feed them to his brood (FN, 333). When he is ten years old, he is completely obsessed by the sandman whose figure he draws constantly; finally, trembling with fear and curiosity, he hides in his father's room in order to see the monster. He is discovered and severely punished by Coppelius, the mysterious stranger with whom his father performs alchemic experiments. Nathanael's most vivid recollection of the scene is a feverish vision of horror. He sees himself in the hands of Coppelius who removes his limbs and seeks to tear out his eyes.

Clara suggests a more rational explanation of the frightful events; she cautions Nathanael against his unbridled imagination, tells him that he has envisioned the horror scenes (FN, 339), and warns him against his tendency to believe in evil powers which inexorably control his fate. She argues that they are projections of his unconscious: "If there is a dark power which adversely and malignantly throws a lure into us and coaxes us onto a dangerous path which we would not have entered otherwise—if there were such a power, it must arise within us, form part of us, become our very self; for only *then* do we believe in it and give it the opportunity it needs to achieve its secret work" (FN, 340). She is especially anguished when Nathanael returns from the university, for she notices that he is no longer capable of controlling his future but instead willingly acquiesces in the dictum of a dark fate (FN, 346). Without understanding she listens to his new mystical, formless poetry and thereby contributes to his alienation. She is shocked into the awareness of impending disaster when he finally succeeds in expressing all his fears in a daring and frightening poem, whose central image is the eye, a rapidly moving circle of fire which destroys him and Clara (FN, 347–48).

This image, which presages Nathanael's insanity, recurs twice in the story. He has a vision of the fiery circle after witnessing a fight between his professor and Coppola over the eyes of Olimpia, the mechanical doll with whom he has fallen in love. Later when he seems cured, and apparently yearns for light and transcendence, he climbs the high tower of city hall with Clara. Looking out over the land he reaches in his pocket only to find a telescope. When he looks by chance at Clara, he sees her too as a doll and tries to murder her. Raging, "Whirl, circle of fire—whirl, circle of fire," he flings himself from the tower while Coppelius threatens from below. In the light of the other tales it becomes evident that Hoffmann in the symbolic use of the eye distinguishes between the clear eye shining with love (Clara, Ulla,

Madelon, Röschen), the eye as symbol of man's harmony with nature and God, and the fear-inspiring broken glance or piercing eyes of Coppola, Euphemie, Aline. Nathanael's fear of losing his eyes is associated from the beginning with circles of fire, which increase in size as the story unfolds until the last one completely engulfs him. Thus he is not only afraid of failing to perceive the world correctly but also of losing his self. For the imagery of the fiery circle reflects the eventual total destruction of his personality center.

Through Clara's love Nathanael could overcome his alienation from the world; he could "open his eyes," see and breathe life into his poetry. His fear of the world, however, especially of the critical judgments of others (FN, 341–42, 348) thrusts him back upon his visions. He finds fulfillment only in his love for Olimpia, a machine which also lacks a personality center: "Only in Olimpia's love can I find my own identity" (FN, 356).[2] His obsession with the telescope further reveals that he is no longer capable of a true experience of nature. Just as the scientists Leuwenhoek and Swammerdamm in *Master Flea* are unable to locate the secrets of life through their telescopes so Nathanael is unable to see reality. The telescope only increases the distortion of his vision.

Subsequently Nathanael's impression of the world resembles ever more a dance of death. The fear-inspiring eye always watches him; a thousand eyes stare at him (FN, 351); death looks at him through Clara's eyes; Coppelius and Coppola merge into one person; their bared teeth and macabre motions are reminiscent of death; even Clara seems a lifeless machine which has to be destroyed; and in a final vision Coppelius, who has grown to huge proportions, stands among a throng of people—all staring at Nathanael until he plunges to his death. The last scene reveals perhaps better than any other that the dimension of evil in the world depends on the observer's perspective. The terror assumes gigantic size for Nathanael, thereby jailing him in a cage constructed by his own fantasy.

In "Councilor Krespel," structured as a suspense story in which the secret is revealed at the end, the reader witnesses the disaster which befalls two people who struggle valiantly to master their destiny.[3] Krespel, though he seems convinced of life's absurdity, tries to reverse the fate of his daughter Antonie and save her life. The lot meted out to Antonie leaves her with the choice either of obeying her father and sacrificing her art or of following her calling, aware that the latter will mean certain death.

Krespel, a lawyer and gifted violinist, is first introduced to the reader as a person who has tried to assert his independence from life. He has built a house which defies tradition; he also ignores conventions and instead of hiding his emotions acts out his anguish through marionette-like leaps into the air. But it soon becomes obvious that his freedom is illusory, that the house has become a prison for him and his daughter. Driven by a passion to discover the secret of music, he has mastered the mechanics of sound production by disassembling old violins and building new ones famous for their beautiful sound. Yet he knows that he has not penetrated the mystery of art. When the truth is unveiled to him through his daughter's death, he is crushed by the burden of his knowledge.

Antonie has barely made her debut as a singer. The supernatural quality of her voice has already given listeners an unsurpassed experience of beauty and aroused the highest admiration in them (S, 36). A physical examination reveals that the beauty of her voice springs from an organic defect and that she will die within six months unless she refrains from singing. Though she is completely dedicated to singing and also engaged to a young composer whom she deeply loves, she follows her father after he has pleaded with her and given her a choice between early death or life with him

51

(S, 48). Her fiancé pursues the two and is permitted to see Antonie after she beseeches her father: "Just let me see him once and then die" (S, 49). When Antonie faints from the exertion of singing again, Krespel frightens off the young man by convincing him that the singing has killed her. Though Krespel's actions are prompted by the noble motive to save his daughter, he suffers from the knowledge that he has played fate and that Antonie can never be really happy again. Hoffmann shows most convincingly how cruelly her father has manipulated her life by establishing an association between her and the cremona violin: both she and the violin are played by a hand which they cannot control. For Antonie, never to sing again is to die a slow death: while she saves her body she cannot fulfill herself in the world by imparting to others a joy of beauty which far surpasses temporal pleasures.

One night Krespel hears faint music, then Antonie's voice; in a clairvoyant moment he sees her in a rapturous embrace with her fiancé, and instinctively knows that she has died (S, 50–51). This vision of her love-death suggests that she, similar to the singer of Donna Anna's part in "Don Juan" (1813), had been deeply inspired by music, had experienced moments of complete harmony and freedom, and now had died in an instant when her spirit had achieved the ultimate union with beauty.[4] Through the sacrifice of her body, Antonie has also achieved selfhood.

Krespel's search for the answer to the enigma of music ends with the death of his daughter. His exclamation, accompanied by almost hellish laughter, "Now I am free again—free—free—hurrah free! Now I shall build no more violins . . ." (S, 42), as well as the calmer statement, "She is gone and the mystery dispelled" (S, 44), underscore the finality of his renunciation. The discovery he made during his vision frees him but simultaneously shatters his world. The true nature of beauty does not reside in the mechanics of its production. And the aesthetic experience of beauty may

lead to death, for the glimpse of cosmic harmony and freedom may be so overpowering that the beholder can no
longer live in the world, whether he regards it like Krespel
as an "insane asylum," or whether he sees it peopled by the
chattering group of philistines who discuss the opera singer's death (FN, 78).

The most striking parallel between Antonie and the
young soprano, identified by the narrator simply as Donna
Anna, lies in the faith of both singers in their ultimate salvation through art.[5] Donna Anna's empathy with music is so
deep that she begins to sense a realm far removed from life,
a realm that cannot be described in words but only dimly
felt: "She said her entire life was music and often she felt
that while singing she could grasp something which was se-
cretly hidden within her" (FN, 71). When the narrator, a
composer whose compositions have expressed the mystery
and passion of her romantic yearning ("the enchanting madness of ever yearning love"), attends a performance of Mozart's *Don Giovanni*, the singer feels his presence and responds to his longing. In the hallucinatory atmosphere
created by her singing, he has an extrasensory experience in
which he meets her in his loge. She expresses her total
affinity with the intentions of his music: "I have sung *you*,
just as *I* am your melodies" (FN, 72). Her presence also inspires him; during the night he begins to comprehend the
true significance of Mozart's opera; the "mysterious realm
of spirits" unveils itself. The following day he hears that
Donna Anna was unconscious during their meeting and died
at two in the morning, precisely at the moment when he felt
her breath. The reader is left to surmise that Donna Anna's
infinite yearning has led to a complete alienation from an
uncomprehending public: "The world remains dead and
cold around me, and while the public applauds a difficult
roulade or an accomplished mannerism, icy hands grip my
blazing heart" (FN, 71). Finally she has fled into the ethereal sphere.

6

The Strange Fairyland

IN THREE FAIRY TALES, *Nutcracker and the King of Mice*, "The Mysterious Child" ["Das fremde Kind," 1817], and *Master Flea*, Hoffmann apparently succeeded in portraying man's self-transcendence. In contrast to the harsh social critical indictment of man's folly in *Little Zaches Called Zinnober* [*Klein Zaches genannt Zinnober*, 1819], the fairy tales have been praised for their imagination, beauty, and idealism.[1] *Master Flea* also elicited considerable scholarly attention for its cutting criticism of the Prussia of Hoffmann's day, which led to the censorship of the book and the elimination of the most offending passages.[2] This critical appraisal of the fairy tales merits serious consideration. They are structured around a clash between good and evil, a contrast between man's ideal and his mundane existence, and present a view of a better world for "those who have the eyes to see it" (S, 252). Presumably they open up a world of beauty to children and idealists who have retained a childlike temperament. In the discussions following their narration in *The Serapion Brethren*, both *Nutcracker and the King of Mice* and "The Mysterious Child" are specifically identified as fairy tales for children which also embody a deep significance (S, 252–54, 472, 510–11). But to read "The Mysterious Child" with the optimism of the last sentence in mind is to overlook the sad but realistic appraisal which precedes it. And the reader who approaches with Marie the fairyland in *Nutcracker and the King of Mice* may at first be overwhelmed by glittering stones, thousands of sparks, and blinding light; yet when he enters the kingdom of the dolls, he begins to realize that appearance is deceptive. For the fairyland is torn by strife and threatened by the same disasters that befall the actual world. While on one level the tales can be enjoyed by children and refer to the established tradition, they also have a distinct, new dimension. They reveal a world in which disorder, strife, violence, and disintegrating personalities have become commonplace. The visions in the fairy tales hold no promise for easy solution. They convey to man the awareness that he must live in his world and seek to improve it.

The action in *Nutcracker and the King of Mice* abounds in conflicts and contrasts of good versus evil, beauty versus ugliness, and the natural versus the artificial. As a result, a dynamic momentum develops which climaxes in the battle between the nutcracker and the mice and is resolved in the victory of the innocence, faith, and determination of a child. The thematic development follows along two lines: one ascends and descends through the world, fairyland, and animal kingdom to focus on man's existential plight; the other resembles an upward spiral which points to the possibility of increased individual and cultural awareness. The plot's action which involves the heroine in much suffering moves in a temporal sequence between antagonistic poles and ends on the same plane where it started. The sequence of events further increases in complexity because the external conflict requires of a naive, sensitive, and imaginative child an existential decision, which must be reached without help from society because the tale's other characters apparently do not understand the necessity for action or lack the strength to commit themselves. Perhaps most disturbing is the ambiguity of the fairyland, where the lack of true essence is glossed over by beautiful appearance and beauty has become deception, because it no longer leads to freedom but conceals the loss of souls and the ever-present fear of its inhabitants.

By employing a subtle irony and the image of the automaton, Hoffmann emphasizes the fact that an escape into a "beautiful fairyland" cannot be equated with self-transcendence. Similarly, the "Fairy Tale of the Hard Nut," related to Marie by her godfather, is not only important for the development of the plot but presents a harsh satire of a life dominated by man's primitive instincts. The images and themes of both the "upper" and the "lower" fairylands illuminate man's situation in the real world in which he is manipulated by forces over which he has no control. Though apparently content, people live in a society in which a true self-realization is no longer possible. In the kingdom of the dolls, the little puppets tremble at the thought of the uncontrollable force of the confectioner, their manipulator. In Pirlipat's court the astronomer valiantly but vainly seeks to fathom the mystery of fate. And in the world only the mysterious godfather Drosselmeier recognizes man's dilemma. The theme is captured perfectly in the figure of the nutcracker himself whose entire life is manipulated and who can only become human with the help of someone else. Thus an interrelationship with Marie is established, for she too comes to understand that she can only realize herself through aiding another human being.

The fairy tale opens with a detailed description of a Christmas Eve celebration in the house of the Stahlbaum family. Among their many presents the children discover an automated toy castle, in which little lifelike figures move on predetermined paths, and a nutcracker shaped like a little man. The children delight in the castle but reject it as a toy because the figures leave no room for imaginative games. Marie, who immediately falls in love with the nutcracker, cries bitterly when her brother Fritz tries him out on some hard nuts and breaks several of his teeth. Nursing him with motherly tenderness she beds him down in the large toy cabinet. Overwhelmed by all the excitement she is about to go to her bedroom when a world of fantasy unfolds before her eyes. She is shocked to see her godfather Drosselmeier straddling the old grandfather clock. Drosselmeier, a slightly eccentric person who delights in building intricate mechanical toys, assumes an important role as guardian of Marie's adventures. Combining good and evil, at once charming and repulsive, he is truly an ambiguous figure. Equally familiar with the actual world and the realm of fantasy, he is at home in neither sphere. Drosselmeier has an intimate knowledge of the spell cast over the nutcracker and, by relating the "Fairy Tale of the Hard Nut," reveals to Marie that she could break it. He almost assumes the role of fate by forcing her and the nutcracker into a situation in which each must make his own decision. He refuses to help the nutcracker in the battle and when he later mends his teeth and jaw he also removes his sword. Furthermore, he rejects Marie's plea for help, pointing out to her that she alone can win the victory.

Marie's initial shock over the transformation of the familiar world gives way to horror when an army of mice springs forth, greets its seven-headed king, and marches into battle against the nutcracker. The reason for the fight remains a mystery to Marie who watches with increasing loathing and fear as the mice attack all the attractive toys which have rallied around the nutcracker. Leveling charges of their excrement and biting the toys to pieces, the mice are about to win when Marie hurls her shoe at their king.

Through her decision to intervene the nutcracker is saved; the vision vanishes and Marie plunges to the floor.

After she awakens sick in bed, Marie cannot be convinced by rational explanations that she had dreamed. Indeed, Drosselmeier's story only strengthens her belief that the nutcracker was her godfather's bewitched nephew and that everything she had witnessed actually happened. She keeps her faith despite the disbelief, laughter, and ridicule of her family and soon learns that her continued apprehension about the nutcracker's safety proves correct. The king of mice visits her nightly and demands tribute in exchange for the nutcracker's life. With a heavy heart she sacrifices her sugar and marzipan dolls until the king's increasingly greedy demands teach her that the voracious appetite of evil is limitless. Once she recognizes the symbolic significance of the mice and comprehends that ugliness will deface beauty and that evil will destroy good unless each is fought, she intervenes consciously in the struggle. She secures a sword for the nutcracker who thereby gains control over his life by killing the king of mice the following night. Thus Marie crosses the two most important stages of her development: she becomes conscious of good and evil and matures from passively suffering for another person to an active decision concerning his and her destiny.

To reward her for her courageous act, the nutcracker, who as a result of her decision has been transformed into the handsome young nephew of Drosselmeier, takes the delighted Marie to his beautiful fairyland. The portrait of this candyland over which both rule after their wedding contains the fairy tale's most disturbing aspects. On the surface candyland seems to be a charmed children's paradise: trees laden with silvery and golden apples, streets of hard candy, brooks brimming with lemonade and orangeade, houses built of chocolate bars and Christmas cookies, dancing shepherds and shepherdesses, quaint little villages where children fish for nuts, and finally a breathtaking capital with a palace of marzipan. Yet, life is threatened from within and without. The dance of the ballet dancers resembles the intricate movements of Drosselmeier's figures, because they are marionettes whose actions are absolutely predictable (S, 241). The villagers, far from being blissful, either suffer from toothache or busily wrap their candy village to protect it against insects, because they cannot escape from the world in which they are condemned to live.

Hoffmann furthermore introduces an element of the irrational into the motions of the candy figurines by instilling into them human fears and hopes. By mimicking the human world their behavior becomes a terrifying reflection of life. And the adult reader whose illusion has already been jolted by the repeated surfeit of sweets sees his own life mirrored in their struggles and conflicts. The existential fear, which is barely hidden behind the sparkling exterior of candyland, culminates in the theme of ultimate consumption which Hoffmann skillfully introduces at the beginning of the fairy tale by creating a scene of Christmas joy around a tree covered with sweets and nuts. The whole world of candy is continuously threatened by forces which seek to annihilate it. Armies of insects attack; the giant "Leckermaul" snaps the roof off the palace and so that he will spare the rest of the residence, is offered an entire section of the town; finally, when the mayor quells an uproar by shouting "Confectioner," it becomes obvious that everyone dreads a fate over which he has no control:

In this land, Confectioner is the name of an unknown but awesome power, which, as the inhabitants believe, can do whatever it wants with man; this is the fate which rules these small gay people, and they are so afraid of it that the slightest mention of the name can incur the greatest tumult, as the Lord Mayor has just proven. No one thinks any longer of earthly things, of the jabbing of ribs and the knocking of heads, but begins to contemplate, saying, "What is man and what will become of him?" [S, 246]

Essentially the population is incapable of facing the great challenge to accept life and rise above its fear of death. Yet, contemplating Marie's marvel and joy as she is guided through fairyland or watching a performance of Tchaikovsky's *Nutcracker* could convince us that she has entered the realm of beauty. This implication generates the greatest ambiguity. If the magic world is identified with beauty, then Hoffmann points to a profound crisis in art. Art has either voluntarily withdrawn from the world into isolation or has been cut off from society. Only those who like Marie retain a childlike vision can hope to perceive it. Furthermore, appearance and play, essential characteristics of art, prove impotent when confronted with the horrible reality of man's situation. Covering agony and sorrow, art has become deception and therefore abets man's spiritual decline.

The "Fairy Tale of the Hard Nut" by motivating the transformation of Drosselmeier's nephew into a nutcracker repeats the basic theme and motifs in a series of variations. The king's passion for sausage, the mouse queen's lust for bacon, even the curse upon Princess Pirlipat to crack and devour nuts incessantly point to the primitive emotions that enchain these figures. Life at court lacks all ideals and resembles that of the mice.

The ironic tone, the many parodies, and the picture of candyland as a paradise mirroring man's world reflect Hoffmann's deep pessimism. To be charmed by the beautiful glitter of this picture is to overlook its tragic dimension. The sparkling frosting poured by the almighty confectioner over the land cannot hide the struggle and plight of its inhabitants. Just as Marie comes of age through her encounters with the different planes of the magic realms, so the reader becomes slowly aware of the deep ambiguity. *Nutcracker and the King of Mice* presents a picture of man's existence in three tableaus which are partially unjust but contain enough truth to be frightening. Drosselmeier's soulless figures and the dancers which move along their predetermined paths reflect a world in which man has become a cog in a machine and is no longer capable of realizing his potential.[3] The ravenous mice and gluttonous court of Pirlipat's father show a world ruled by instincts. Candyland, finally, mirrors a world in which man is in the process of becoming but is still dominated by materialistic creeds and primitive fears. All three portraits bring man's caged existence into sharp focus. Yet through Marie's action Hoffmann also presents in the fairy tale a specific solution for man in his search for existential commitment: by conquering her fear, retaining faith in her vision, and unselfishly helping another person, she transforms the nutcracker and succeeds in transcending the limitations of the world.

"The Mysterious Child," apparently identified by the narrator as "more pious and childlike" than the fairy tale of the nutcracker (S, 472) because it is less ironic and delights in stark, simple contrast, opens with an idyllic, pastoral scene. Two children, Felix and Christlieb, who have been permitted to grow up in complete innocence, spend most of their time playing in the forest. Suddenly their lives are disrupted by the arrival of distant cousins, children who appear to be almost automata in their movements and modern computers in their ability to feed back a wealth of information acquired from their tutor (S, 478–79). After a few hours they disappear, but not before they have left unusual presents and their father has promised to send a tutor for Felix and Christlieb. As a result of the visit the children's lives are profoundly altered.

The presents, especially a beautiful doll and the automated figures of a hunter and a harpist, induce the children to forego their usual games in the forest. But the charm of the toys quickly fades when the children take them into the woods the following day. Suddenly they seem lifeless and after some rough playing are broken by the children who then cast the useless toys away. Yet the next day Felix and Christlieb seem incapable of enjoying their old games. They are reminded of the toys, even long to be as educated as their cousins who obviously never would have broken the figures, and finally begin to cry in despair (S, 485). At this moment the mysterious child comes to play with them, opens their eyes to the hidden beauty in the world, and inspires them by calling forth a vision of nature animated by lovely fairies and elves.

The interpretation of the subsequent action in which Hoffmann portrays a continuous struggle between the child and Magister Tinte (alias gnome Pepser) for the souls of the children will obviously depend on one's view of the child's symbolic significance.[4] Explanations have been so different because in the child Hoffmann has created an open symbol which calls forth varied associations. Still, the fairy tale leaves little doubt that the child awakens the imagination of Felix and Christlieb and comforts their existential anguish. It also explains to them the dangers of wild flights of fancy (S, 494) and relates how it is threatened on earth by its mother's foe, the gnome who attacked the beautiful realm and almost succeeded in covering it with black ink. Pepser's actions at the court of the child's mother prove him a sworn enemy of imagination, beauty, and the cult of nature (S, 494–96). He looks upon nature as a source to be cultivated and exploited ("rather than play with them, he wanted to devour the poor, tame animals"). Small wonder he abhors the children's view of nature. When he arrives in the shape of Magister Tinte as tutor for Felix and Christlieb, he ridicules them and later on a walk in the forest begins to attack their environment (S, 499–501). Thereupon the children drive him away with the help of their father. Consequently the struggle extends beyond a mere conflict between imagination and reason, belief and doubt, to one between a charmed view of nature as man's friend and a view of nature as a useful material object.

Several problems related to the conclusion of the fairy tale are usually ignored by critics. After the children free themselves, the forest remains lifeless, but the discarded mechanical figures arise to frighten them (S, 506–07). After being exposed to the gnome's perspective, the children have lost their innocence forever. They are now fearful and overcome by longing for the former state of bliss. Soon they experience the death of their father, who before his end recalls how he too had known the beautiful child when he was their age and how their story had so affected him that a boundless yearning was breaking his heart (S, 509). A frightening death scene in which the children cry for their father is followed by the loss of the home, claimed by the rich cousin, and their departure into the strange world. Just before they leave the forest, the child appears in a final flush of light to remind them that it will be with them in their dreams if they keep their faith (S, 510). Since the child's apparition is limited to the adult's dreams or the hour when he faces death, the reader has to assume that the gnome's perspective governs the world. Perhaps even more frightening is the picture of a world devoid of imagination and ruled by mechanical toys.

In *Little Zaches Called Zinnober* the ironic and tragicomic elements, already noticeable in the previously considered fairy tales, begin to dominate the structure of the narrative. Certainly *Little Zaches* no longer evinces the "quiet tone and innocence of the presentation" which Hoffmann praised in Tieck's fairy tales.[5] The imaginative-magic sphere clearly functions as a foil which draws attention to man's plight and folly. Indeed fairies, elves, and magicians were abolished by edict when the wise ruler of the little land began to civilize his subjects. By introducing the "Enlightenment" he modernized his state, that is, had trees cut down, roads built, canals dug, everyone vaccinated, and thus effectively eliminated nearly all the old poetic charm (SW, 16–18). To prevent a revolution, the ruler permitted a few fairies to remain but under strict orders to become "useful members" of society so that rational people would not be confused with visions of beauty. In a biting satire, reminiscent of *Gulliver's Travels*, Hoffmann attacks the social injustice which pervades every aspect of life, the state's corrupt political system which favors the incompetent, and a legal system that provides no justice.[6]

A few students and other romantic persons still believe in beauty, magic, and the arts, although the scientific studies of Mosch Terpin make such heresy almost impossible. He has not only classified and catalogued nature (SW, 22) but also the celestial sphere (SW, 71). When one of the fairies who have been associated with imagination and beauty intervenes in the world, it comes as a shock to see her glorify a totally worthless creature. While Hoffmann obviously needed an especially ugly figure like the gnome Zaches to bring out the discrepancy behind the actual situation and the deceit practiced in the state, the function of art also becomes suspect. Hoffmann frequently reasoned that a true work of art had to free man from the shackles of his environment and reveal to him a vision of ennobled humanity. "There is no higher purpose for art than to arouse in man the desire that frees his entire being from all earthly torment, from all the depressing pressures of everyday life as from unclean cinders, thus uplifting him so that he may perceive the divine, or even come in contact with it." [7] But the charm bestowed upon Zaches only deceives people into attributing to him the excellence shown by others. Again the question arises whether the illusion of art does not become outright deception in a society which has lost faith in its ideals. For lack of substance the artist could glorify the idol of a period, as occurs when the fairy Rosabelverde [Rosenschön] casts her spell over Zaches. He subsequently rises to the top governmental post in the state because he follows the general maxim: Appear to be more than you are. Or the artist could play with forms like the great magician Prosper Alpanus who drives through the forest in a harmoniously sounding chariot resplendent in fantastic colors and at the end of the fairy tale disappears in the sky on a flaming rainbow, leaving man to his lot (SW, 100).

Neither Zaches's life and rise to power nor his absurd death in a bedpan (SW, 90–91) evoke much sympathy in the reader. At first his future seems to be tragic because it is predetermined by his birth and his extreme ugliness. But when the spell transforms him into a charming personality in the eyes of the world, he never attempts to live up to the high expectation of those around him. He remains psychologically as unbalanced as he is physically deformed.[8] The conclusion of the fairy tale resembles the last scene in *The Golden Pot*. The student Balthasar who has fought with Zaches gains his bride, inherits a poetic fief from Prosper Alpanus, and, inspired by him, becomes a good poet. Yet, this charming vision, of which the poet himself says "Isn't it more delightful to have a happy wedding than a sad funeral at the end?" does not invalidate the extended panorama of man's painful existence: that of Little Zaches's mother who is born to misfortune; of the citizens of the state who are deceived by their government; of the students who are mystified by Mosch Terpin; of the prince who is duped by his ministers; and of all who are deluded by Zaches. The truly tragic figures of the fairy tale, however, are the people who have no recourse against the whims of their government and, though they seem eager to rebel, are easily pacified (SW, 90).[9]

As in other tales, Hoffmann is primarily concerned with man's suffering and folly, that is, with the purely human situation which he portrays in *Little Zaches* with humor and detachment. In *Princess Brambilla* [*Prinzessin Brambilla*, 1821] which he called a *capriccio*, the light touch of the artist is even more evident; there dreams, visions, and the magic realm have been completely integrated into the actual world by enshrouding the action in a prolonged carnival scene. The result is a supra-real dance of masks which could be characterized by the motto: Salvation for the artist in particular and his audience in general can be found in the magic opera. The action slowly reveals how Giglio Fava, an actor of highly pathetic roles, learns that a comedy can express the most profound thoughts and give man an experience of intellectual freedom. As part of his maturing process Giglio Fava also falls in love and achieves true selfhood through his experience.

Whether one sees the dance of masks as an expression of pessimism and hears in the laughter the outcry of nihilism or assumes that the *capriccio* is a humorous play by a gifted artist seems to depend almost more on the reader's disposition than on his conscientious reading.[10] Certainly, sufficient evidence can be found in the story to support the view that the main characters are healed through the experience of humor in art. For instance, the "Story of King Ophioch and Queen Liris," which presages the final events, reveals how two persons are healed through the contemplation of art. The king is deeply saddened by the realization that man's increased consciousness has destroyed his previous unconscious but harmonious existence in which he rested on the breast of mother nature (SW, 251). The queen, untouched by the king's anxiety, nevertheless reminds him of his plight because her constant, senseless laughter tells him that modern man can never return to a previous state without sacrificing an important part of his personality. The two are healed after the great magician Hermod creates a beautiful fountain in which they see an inverted picture of the totality of nature and themselves (SW, 256). The contemplation of a concentrated and yet humorously inverted image of life provides an aesthetic experience of a new harmony, one based on the conscious recognition of man's situation.

If swift, often hurried motion characterizes Giglio Fava who dances and tumbles through the action, then contemplation and withdrawal are distinctive features of Peregrinus Tyss's stance toward the world. The opening scenes of *Master Flea*, bizarre and grotesque in their total effect, show Tyss hiding from what he considers the absurdity and cruelty of life. Preoccupied with his fantasies, he behaves in a manner incompatible with his age: On Christmas Eve a highly excited boy shouts with joy as he discovers the presents from his parents, plays, rides a cockhorse, and falls from it; then, suddenly the reader discovers that the boy is thirty-six years old, has bought his own presents, and celebrates with an old housekeeper, since his parents died long ago (SW, 677–79). As the fairy tale unfolds, the fixed point of Tyss's eccentricity is brought into sharper focus. He has retained a childlike faith in man, is repulsed by the materialistic values of his class (SW, 684–85), and prefers to live in a world of fantasy, governed by love, compassion, and honor. The sections in which Hoffmann contrasts this utopia with the existing social order contain not only his most militant criticism of man's spiritual decline but also a sharp thrust leveled against Tyss.[11] In a moment of special irritation Tyss learns from his friend Pepusch that his retreat from an unscrupulous society is a delusion and he hears his charity and social sensibility condemned as lacking in all true understanding for the vast suffering surrounding him (SW, 739–40). Pepusch denounces the fear of the world and the measure of egotism which Tyss reveals in his activities.

The ensuing action revolves around the question of whether Tyss can become fully conscious of his motives and still adhere to his ethical standards. In the process his ethical code is tested to see whether it is strong enough to endure in the world and persuasive enough to foster a spiritual rebirth of others. Flung into the world, he loses his childlike innocence, is tempted by violent passions, and confronted with the choice between the flea, a grotesque but innocent creature seeking his protection, and a beautiful girl offering her love at the price of the little monster (SW, 695–98, 715–30). Tyss finally wins the struggle between the ethos of renunciation and instinctive, immediate gratification, highlighted by the theme "altruism must conquer passion" (SW,

768, 782, 785, 794–95). In contrast to his achievement his antagonist Knarrpanti utterly fails because his perception of the world is colored by his egotism, and all of his actions are prompted by base motives (SW, 736 ff., 751 ff.). Though this development suggests that Tyss is exposed to the world in order to realize his innate potential and achieve a greater consciousness of his motivation (the traditional education-of-man theme), it veils an important aspect of his growth.

When he receives the magic lens from Master Flea, he not only perceives the incongruity between appearance and reality, that is, between the dignified, generous overt behavior of men and their hidden, selfish thoughts, but has also acquired the power of solving the mysteries of nature (SW, 733–34, 742–44, 755–59). It is no coincidence that the two "scientists" Leuwenhoek and Swammerdamm, who try to master nature, covet the lens that holds forth the promise of ultimate knowledge. To possess it is to fulfill the dream of autonomy. What the two do not realize is that the penetration of nature's secrets may perhaps satisfy biological needs but will also create new ones and will not help mankind as long as the knowledge thus gained serves only for nature's further exploitation as well as for man's enslavement (SW, 719–21). By satirizing the puppetlike movements of the two "scientists," Hoffmann points to their intellectual captivity and spiritual void (SW, 746). As Tyss learns, knowledge not tempered by love for man remains sterile and leads to a profound spiritual disharmony: "Your heart has remained dead and rigid . . . You believed that you were contemplating the great, holy miracles of nature in pious admiration and devotion, but because you irreverently sought to penetrate to the innermost core of the essence of these miracles, you yourself have destroyed the devotion. And the knowledge to which you aspired was a phantom which deceived you like curious, prying children" (SW, 811). When Tyss reflects upon the power of the lens, he begins to comprehend that it will eventually destroy his faith in man and, by interfering with the meeting of "I" and "Thou," prevent his true self-realization:

"What?" he asked himself. "A person who probes into the most secret thoughts of his brothers—doesn't that ill-fated gift call upon him the terrifying fate of the Wandering Jew who roved through the most colorful bustle of the world, as through a gloomy, inhospitable desert without joy, without hope, without pain, in mute indifference which is the culmination of despair? Always hoping again, always trusting anew, and forever bitterly deceived, must not distrust, evil suspicion, hate, and revenge begin to nest in his soul and devour every trace of a truly human nature, which is expressed in mild trust and pious friendliness? No! . . . I want to see you as my friend; I want to be as good to you as I can; I shall open my heart to you, because it will benefit me." [SW, 805–806]

Tyss, willing to believe that man has the potential to be good, rejects the lure of cognition in favor of the ancient wisdom of love. Hoffmann sums up his victory succinctly through an extraordinary vision: Tyss is transformed into the ruler of peace, who holds the sacred lotus instead of a scepter and whose love, symbolized by the heart set aflame by the mystic almandine, conquers and transcends all other emotions (SW, 809). The lotus symbol further confirms that Tyss was successful in his struggle for self-realization.[12]

Unfortunately this vision is so lofty that it remains a postulate. Indeed, it appears as if Hoffmann himself no longer dares to believe in it. The scene is interrupted by a grotesque incident designed to destroy the reader's illusion. First, the old maid Aline, dressed as the Queen of Golkonda, appears and begins to play with the two "scientists" who have shriveled to the size of dolls. Singing a lullaby she rocks them in a cradle (SW, 811–12). Then Master Flea is suddenly overwhelmed by his natural desire "and jumped, whooping loudly, 'True love remains eternally young!' with a single leap onto Dörtjen's neck" (SW, 812). And the apparently charming idyl of family love which concludes the fairy tale ridicules bourgeois life and is incommensurate with the existential dilemma experienced by Tyss. The reader is again left with the picture of a struggle which continues in the world, for Tyss's victory amounts to a gentle defeat.

The exuberance found in the fairy tales hides a tragic view of life. Marie and Tyss actively struggle for self-realization and surmount all obstacles by adhering to their values. They are not passive victims of fear. They succeed in establishing a meaningful relationship between themselves and others. But although we can understand Marie's vision and identify with the values of Tyss, we cannot rationally support a frosted image of the world, and we scorn the Biedermeier paradise which awaits Tyss. The children Felix and Christlieb are driven from Eden but, by remaining faithful to their beliefs, retain a spark of the beauty which their childhood held before its destruction. They will live in a world that is easily deceived by the gnome Zaches, a world in which imagination is hiding, and which is slowly taken over by mechanical toys. Perhaps the most important technique used by Hoffmann to reveal to us the despair in life is his presentation of the struggle between good and evil against a broad panorama of a world in ceaseless conflict, a world inhabited by helpless fools, puppets, and a few dreamers. And while *Princess Brambilla* holds forth the promise of an aesthetic rebirth of man, a true spiritual reform remains but a faint hope. For the explicitly grotesque figure of little Zaches reflects the spiritual situation of man as much as the Atlantis envisioned by Anselmus or Balthasar represents a human ideal.

71

7

Visions of Compulsion and Death—
The Infernal Fairy Tales

DESPITE THE FRIGHTENING PORTRAIT of the world depicted by the works considered so far, they do not invite us to escape into dreams, for the poet's seductive whisper to play with him in the clouds is invariably followed by a plunge to earth. The tragic struggle for self-realization challenges the reader to work for a true reform of society. These narratives show Hoffmann's deep awareness of the fact that man not only possesses the potential to embrace ideals and yearn for beauty but is also susceptible to the lure of evil. In the tales "Automata" ["Die Automate," 1814], "Ignaz Denner" (1816), "The Vow" ["Das Gelübde," 1817], "The Mines of Falun" ["Die Bergwerke zu Falun," 1819], and "Mademoiselle de Scudéry" ["Das Fräulein von Scuderi," 1820], however, Hoffmann probes into the dark forces confronting man from within, portrays the profound discord of fallen man, and explores the psychology of evil. The world of beauty recedes ever further into the background, though the challenge to man not to succumb to the demonic forces which lurk within him remains.

What fascinates Hoffmann is the ugliness of a world which has rejected all ethical norms as well as man's deep-seated fears, his thoughts, drives, and the desires which are repressed by civilized society. The will to portray man's unconscious motivations and thoughts manifests itself in several stylistic features such as a stream of consciousness technique which records thoughts, dreams, and the perception of real occurrences without distinction. The description of reality becomes less precise and charged with emotional qualities. Repeatedly used linguistic clichés point not only to a devaluation of reality but also to some of the characters' stereotyped barren conceptions of the world.[1] Different levels of awareness are mirrored in different experiences of time; for instance, while the monk Medardus suffers in a preconscious, sometimes insane condition, his world, like that of Benjy in Faulkner's *The Sound and the Fury*, becomes timeless. Past and present occurrences fuse into an eternal now. When he seems conscious, his perception of time corresponds to the imaginary course of events. Ideas and thoughts assume representational shapes in alter ego projections, in figures stepping out of paintings, and in concrete descriptions of martyr scenes or the loss of one's shadow. But above all Hoffmann succeeds in symbolizing man's terror in scenes of sudden arrest or torture, scenes in which children are stabbed, the bones of victims crushed, their flesh torn, and in which the pain becomes unendurable. The stories that convey to the reader an intensified perception of man's unconscious form part of a development in literature which began with romanticism and is still in process, a development in which man's unconscious, psychological processes, his primitive instincts, and every thought no matter how trite or ridiculous become subjects for artistic representation.[2] Whether Hoffmann felt that such art would free man and increase his consciousness of himself or limit his vision cannot be ascertained. The "psychological narrations" give the impression of an absurd rather than a tragic view of existence, because the characters either passively await their fate or suffer a senseless, arbitrary doom.

"Automata" contains the most detailed discussion and explicit rejection of machines and marionettes (S, 330).[3] In contrast to Kleist, Hoffmann sees no gracefulness in any life-imitating mechanism. To him machines lack soul and will. Since their actions are completely predetermined, Hoffmann employs mechanical figures to symbolize a life which is manipulated by forces beyond human control. "I could imagine that it might be possible to enable figures to dance quite graciously by means of a secret mechanism within them. They also should dance with people and execute difficult movements so that a live dancer holds a wooden lady and swings with her back and forth. Could you watch this for one minute without horror?" (S, 346) Hoffmann singles out intricate musical machines for his most vitriolic attack, whereas he seems rather intrigued by the possibility of electronic music (S, 345–50). The events and the theoretical discussions prompted by such mechanisms show how he abhors and yet is strangely fascinated by a human existence of passive acquiescence to fate.

In the story Hoffmann interweaves a dream sequence with the rational debates of two friends. Swept along with everyone else in the city, Ludwig and Ferdinand go to see a machine which mysteriously seems capable not only of answering the most difficult questions but also of predicting the future. It seems as if "young and old, rich and poor" throng to the oracle because they lack inner security and look for support in the machine's mysterious and alarming revelations, the truth of which is half-hidden, half-revealed (S, 332). When Ferdinand fearfully and hesitantly approaches the machine and inquires whether he will ever see his beloved again, he hears that he will lose her. Wounded to the core, he tries to decipher the meaning of the ominous prediction. All efforts to find an answer to the riddle in the intricate mechanism of the machine have to be abandoned. Even the suggestion that it might be manipulated by a person possessing extrasensory powers (S, 343) proves erroneous.

The reader slowly becomes aware that Ferdinand is looking for an answer which is deeply embedded within himself. He has encountered the woman he loves only once in a dream vision and then painted an idealized miniature portrait of her that he carries on an amulet around his neck (S, 334–38). To him the picture has become a symbol of inspiration; to find the girl in the actual world would mean to lose an essential part of himself; therefore he fears such an encounter and is ultimately relieved when he realizes the nature of his ideal (S, 353). That the machine only echoes man's secret hopes and fears, that the whisper of the automaton is in fact the voice of the questioner's own unconscious finally begins to dawn upon Ludwig after his friend's deeply disturbing experience (S, 353–54).

Fragmented pieces of observation, projections of unconscious fears, dreams, and conscious reflections blend into a dynamic sequence of events in "A New Year's Eve Adventure" ["Die Abenteuer der Sylvester-Nacht," 1815]. In this story Hoffmann warns his readers, moreover, that the narrator-protagonist cannot cut the web spun by his unconscious and does not distinguish between actual and imaginary events (FN, 256, 283). Haunted by the fear of being alone, by memories of lost happiness, and by the recognition of his mortality, the narrator rushes through the streets. As he hastens from party to winecellar and from there to a hotel room, momentary impressions call forth associations in his mind. Inspired by a painting of temptation or a vision of his ideal, he first experiences moments of bliss with his "love" Julie. The dreamlike quality of the encounter is several times briefly disrupted by her glance which frightens, almost terrorizes him (FN, 259). Suddenly music—he holds her hand—he knows for his good she must stay, for she alone inspires his creativity—her husband calls—and a strange woman leaves him (FN, 260). He rages on, descends into the winecellar, and is inspired by literary motifs. Soon he converses with Peter Schlemihl whom he has never "seen but frequently imagined" and with a stranger who has lost his mirror-image.

The three recognize their disharmony, suffering, and finally each other: the narrator who sacrificed his self, Schlemihl who lost his shadow, and Erasmus Spikher who gave away his image. Soon fear disrupts their conversation. Again the narrator hurries away, takes a hotel room where he meets Spikher in bed, has visions of him writing, and then either imagines or consciously recognizes that everything he has seen was a beautiful arrangement of candy figures in a window (FN, 265–68). When he awakens he finds a manuscript which purports to explain the disaster that befell Spikher, but which really mirrors his own fate, giving the reader a renewed insight into the protagonist's shattered self. In the account, "The Story of the Lost Reflection," Spikher travels to Italy, meets Giulietta, an angelic woman, and is overpowered by the feeling that she is the incarnation of his yearning for beauty (FN, 271). Seized by an insane passion for her and willing to risk his soul, he is confronted by visions of evil. Satan offers help. Spikher murders an admirer of Giulietta and, forced to flee, cannot tear himself away from her until he has left his image in her arms. Later he is terror-stricken by the idea that his loss will be discovered and tempted to murder wife and child for Giulietta. The visions disappear when he finally conquers his lust.

Spikher's emotions, excesses, and suffering parallel those of the narrator. Indeed Spikher's exclamation upon first seeing Giulietta characterizes the emotions of both: "Yes, it is *you*, I have always loved *you*, *you* angel! I have seen you in my dreams, *you* are my happiness, my salvation, my ideal!" (FN, 271). As a result of their love, their "shimmering dream-ego" becomes independent and they experience a loss of an essential part of the self. To view the resulting identity crisis only in the light of Spikher's fate would be misleading. He sacrificed himself to a phantom without experiencing a truly redeeming love. The narrator offers himself to a vision of beauty which continues to inspire him and to give him a ray of hope in the darkness of his turmoil.

The compulsion which endangers the free development of man's potential assumes demonic proportions in "The Primogeniture" ["Das Majorat," 1817], "The Vow," and "The Mines of Falun." In "The Primogeniture" Hoffmann presents two distinct actions: the events experienced by Theodor, the narrator, and the chronicle of Count Roderich's family which Theodor's great-uncle relates to him. Aside from the external connection which is established when Theodor falls in love with the countess, the two stories have the same focal point in the thematic juxtaposition of enslavement versus self-determination. The question raised is whether man is completely in the hands of demonic forces or capable of making just and right decisions. Several events, such as the tragedy which befalls the family, the death of Seraphine, and Theodor's love which almost leads to a catastrophe, would support the view that an inscrutable power rules man's destiny.[4] The great-uncle, a powerful figure who counsels the members of the family and actually saves Theodor, concludes upon contemplating the destruction of the people he served so well that the mystery remains unsolved: "It is the essential point that I cannot explain, that no one can express" (FN, 528). The family chronicle, however, proves to be an extensive account of man's weakness, of hate and primitive passion. Hoffmann's characterization of the old count and his two sons is certainly not designed to awaken the reader's compassion.

Their failure in life springs from their own obsessions and evil deeds which reach a climax when Hubert conspires with the old servant Daniel to kill his brother (FN, 557). The final chapter in the chronicle is written when Roderich, the last heir of the estate, and his wife Seraphine meet Theodor.

In contrast to their ancestors, Roderich and Seraphine are depicted as noble characters who suffer a fate which they cannot understand. They fear the past and the atmosphere of the castle in which the crime has been committed. As soon as Theodor arrives he too is strangely affected by the surroundings. As he reads Schiller's "Geisterseher" that night, he suddenly feels a ghost moving through the room. The scratching sounds, the steps, and the breeze cannot simply be attributed to his vivid imagination, for his great-uncle not only believes his story but also succeeds the following night in banning the ghost of Daniel, who had killed his master and later died of shock in that room. However superior the reader may feel to the experience, it enables him to participate in the fictional events and, above all, to comprehend Hoffmann's intention.[5] For the ghost, both real and imagined, assumes fateful proportions in Seraphine's fantasy. Her fear reminds Roderich of the past and the unresolved question whether he is morally responsible for Daniel's death, despite the fact that the man had been a murderer.

The final disaster occurs when Seraphine is killed in an accident. The picture of the sled pulled by the shying horses conveys the impression of speeding life which flings Seraphine out of the cage onto the bright open field (FN, 558). Her cry, "The old man—the old man is chasing us," and the great-uncle's remark, "Evil fate, an awesome power, has reached even *her*, the lovely lady" would indicate that she was trapped. How ardently she desired to break out of her castle-prison becomes most evident in the brief moments of joy she experienced with Theodor. Sensitive, interested in poetry and music, an accomplished singer and pianist, he has fallen in love with her. But his romantic, "knightly love" soon becomes a compulsion. (FN, 503, 508, 515 ff.) She responds to his yearning; while he plays the piano and she sings, a vision of beauty opens before her eyes (FN, 509, 515). One evening she confides to him her fears of the curse that seems to hang over her life. By relating his own experience and by softly playing a canzone of St. Steffani, Theodor conveys to her the feeling of freedom. The evening ends with a scene in which reality and imagination blend into a vision of love: "How did it happen that I knelt before her, that she yielded to me and while I embraced her a long, radiant kiss burned my lips?" (FN, 516). Yet fear and intoxication prove more powerful than the aesthetic love experience. She begins to be haunted by the vision of Daniel, perhaps an indication of her guilt feeling (FN, 524). Theodor, driven to the brink of madness, rages in the forest. He escapes disaster when his great-uncle, realizing the danger, departs with him the next morning. Though we are encouraged by the great-uncle's decisive action and the recognition that the old count, his sons, and Daniel were responsible for their misfortunes, we suffer with Seraphine and Roderich. They face an incomprehensible world and gripped by an apparently implacable fate seek in vain to fulfill themselves.

A study of the structure of the narrative, the major motif and themes, discloses that in this tale Hoffmann uses the traditional elements of the fairy tale but in an inverted form. He obfuscates the stark contrast and separation between good and evil. Instead of the anticipation of a happy ending he arouses a feeling of impending disaster. The motif of Prince Charming who comes to awaken Sleeping Beauty is transformed: Theodor cannot free Seraphine but intensifies her fear instead. Finally, the theme of liberation is reversed to one of enslavement. Thus Hoffmann has actually created the "infernal fairy tale" which deals with man's existential anguish and the suffering of those who face a wretched, absurd world.

With minor variations, such as that of feminine doubling in virgin and vampire and the motif of beauty and the beast, Hoffmann continues the same theme in "The Mystery of the Deserted House" ["Das öde Haus," 1817]. The story employs ambiguity, contrasts, dream fragments, and pieces of observation to show how a demonic force shatters the narrator's mind. Theodor, the narrator, describes his compulsive love which takes the form of the urge to unearth the secret of a sinister house. Prompted by the contrast between the shabby structure and the stately appearance of all other homes on the street, Theodor begins to daydream and visualizes a story that casts him as the heroic rescuer of an imprisoned maiden. He rejects all rational explanations. Later when he sees a reflection of the imagined girl in his mirror, he can no longer differentiate between actual and imagined events. Driven by the mysterious vision and spurred by the wish to free the beautiful woman, he enters the house one night only to be spellbound not by beauty but by an insane countess. She is held captive and has been frequently enchained, even tortured, by her servant, a gnomish Charon (FN, 466–67). The narrator, horrified by the recognition that his compulsion will drive him insane, decides to seek medical help and eventually frees himself when he becomes acquainted with the countess' tragic history. Yet, even then he does not fully understand what demonic forces seized him, except that a psychic predisposition (FN, 473) might have destroyed him.[6] By suggesting a medical explanation for the narrator's hallucinations, Hoffmann erases some of the ambiguity, limits the reader's capacity for further reflection, and detracts from the major theme and the image of the trap. In general the story is not as well executed as "The Primogeniture."

The themes of love and destruction as well as the image of the cage recur in "The Vow." The story has invited comparisons with Kleist's "Die Marquise von O. . . ." and has been judged as inferior.[7] Despite the many parallels a comparison is not revealing, because the two works differ in basic conception. Kleist's heroine rises above the events that seem to destroy her and thus masters her destiny. Hoffmann's heroine is totally shattered and destroyed by the incongruity between her vision and reality. The plot is stark and clear: after the insurrection following the first partition of Poland, Stanislaus, a freedom fighter, returns to the girl he plans to marry. Hermenegilda, a girl of great beauty and intellect who is impulsive to the point of being irrational, rejects him because he and his friends did not succeed in liberating Poland. After he has left, she deeply regrets her action and her yearning for him soon becomes obsessive. At this moment a younger cousin of Stanislaus arrives. Their resemblance is so startling that Hermenegilda mistakes him for Stanislaus. Affected by her feelings, Xaver develops a love for her which becomes an insane passion (FN, 573). One evening, while she envisions being married to her faraway friend, Xaver takes advantage of her. She becomes pregnant, still convinced that she had been with Stanislaus. Xaver explains his deception, offers his love, and begs her to marry him, but the truth completely shatters her confidence in man. "She leaped up with a heart-rending cry, a cry no longer human but resembling the piercing wail of a wild animal and while her body writhed in agony, stared at the count with blazing eyes" (FN, 585).

She renounces the world and secludes herself in a room resembling a cell to give birth to a child. As if she had not suffered enough, Xaver returns after the child is born and in a singularly horrifying confrontation tears the boy from his mother's arms. In the ensuing struggle Xaver rips the veil from Hermenegilde's face and looks at a white mask. The scene clearly reveals the poet's intentions. Hermenegilda, through her vow never to show her face again, has actually become a symbol for Everyman and her cries of pain reflect the suffering of man (FN, 566). Though she had originally become a victim of her own emotion, the outrageous betrayal gives universal significance to her despair. Again the story focuses on the by now familiar themes and motifs, but is unsurpassed as a stark picture of betrayal.

In the representation of compulsion, however, Hoffmann succeeds far better in "The Mines of Falun." Like many of his narrations this story can be interpreted as portraying a central conflict between man's demonic vision and reality. According to this view the hero Elis Fröbom is driven into a mine by the romantic yearning to discover the mystery of earth only to find death on his wedding day. But "The Mines of Falun," like most of the narratives considered so far, can be read on more than one level.[8] Structurally, it is once again an infernal fairy tale: Hoffmann inverts the motif of the young hero who climbs to the top of a mountain of glass, gains his princess, and lives happily ever after. In Hoffmann's version, the hero descends to the core of the mountain in search of the secret of life, the mysterious red almandine, but discovers the ultimate truth—death. Indeed, the themes of love and compulsion, self-realization and captivity are woven into a symbolic narration of man's confrontation with death on his journey into his unconscious.

Elis Fröbom begins his voyage while his comrades joyously dance and drink. He withdraws quietly from the boisterous scene and mourns the loss of his mother, the only person he had loved and who had always waited for his return from the sea (S, 171–74). When he expresses the wish to die, he suddenly sees the figure of an old miner, a figure strangely familiar and comforting (S, 174). In the ensuing dialog the miner, who virtually orders Elis to overcome his indecision, gives direction to his vague feelings and premonitions by commanding him to look for truth in the mines of Falun: "It seems quite possible that at the bottom of a mine and in the faint light of a lamp man may become increasingly clairvoyant and gaining in strength he may see in the marvelous stones a reflection of the secrets hidden above the clouds" (S, 176). He then proceeds to paint a picture of a magic world intensely fascinating to Elis who feels simultaneously exhilarated and oppressed by the experience because he fears the strange world and yet suspects that he has been there before with the miner. By contrasting the symbolic landscape of metal and stone with the sun-bathed sea, Hoffmann introduces the struggle between the death wish and the yearning for life. That night the vision recurs in a dream to Elis but is transformed into an image of seduction inviting him to come down. He again feels joy and fear. He yearns for the hidden secrets of this world, sees in a flash the universal earth-mother guarding the mysteries of life and death, beholds the old miner, a figure of molten mineral and of gigantic proportions who suddenly warns him of danger, and his rejoicing turns into terror (S, 178). After a brief vision of life calling from above, an inward force compels him to glance downward again. He awakens, deeply and lastingly affected by his dream. After reliving the same conflict during a daydream, Elis is ready to follow his inner voice. Both the old miner and the temptress in the earth are of demonic ambiguity. They resemble a Greek chtonic deity whose voice calls out to life. They remind the hero of his origin, demand action, lure him with the secret of self-knowledge, and warn him of the consequences of his search.

Beckoned and guided by the old man, he arrives at his destination only to be overwhelmed by the sudden fear of death when he sees the huge mine as a terrifying trap (S, 181). He decides to leave immediately but forgets his plan when he meets Ulla Dahlsjö, whose eyes promise light, health, and life. Thus Elis has arrived at the crossroads of his journey. He becomes a miner but looks toward life, eager to be greeted by Ulla when he leaves the shaft. One day the vision of the old miner returns to warn him not to forget the true nature of his search in his love for Ulla. Elis threatens him and rejects the idea. Yet when his love is tested that day, he makes no attempt to save it. Instead he runs in wild desperation back to the mine and, for the first time since meeting Ulla, by concentrating with all his power upon the inner world, he begins to see its mysteries (S, 190–91). Told later that he can marry Ulla he again struggles with himself but resolves his torment on the wedding day by leaving life. Looking for the secret of existence, the secret of his own heart, he descends to the core of the earth and finds death (S, 194).

When the miner had beckoned previously, Elis had always experienced a sensation strangely compounded of terror and joy. In his final hours, however, he embraces death without fear. Yet the true significance of his search remains veiled to him. In searching for the secret of existence within himself, he fails to see that it was revealed to him in Ulla's love. The warm red light he hoped to find in the almandine glowed in her heart. After fifty lonely years of faithful waiting, Ulla too is rewarded with her ultimate truth: death while embracing the rediscovered body of the man she had loved so much. The old woman's subdued weeping echoes the despair of all victims of life. Elis Fröbom's journey had long been ended before the great trap released his body only so that it could fall to dust. He found death before life. What remains is a picture of suffering and nothingness.

Elis and Ulla bowed to an elemental force of the universe. Others, notably Maria in "The Magnetizer" ["Der Magnetiseur," 1814], Andres and his family in "Ignaz Denner" (1816), and Angela in "Gambler's Luck" ["Spielerglück," 1820], become helpless victims in the hands of evil or face it uncomprehendingly as do Olivier Brusson and Madelon in "Mademoiselle de Scudéry." "The Magnetizer" reflects the intense fascination felt by Hoffmann and his contemporaries for magnetism, mesmerism, self-induced hallucinations, and dreams.[9] Hoffmann was especially attracted to magnetism because hypnotized persons seem to

lose all control over their actions. The narration depicts
three events which have as a common theme the use and
abuse of hypnotic power. The first story within the tale explores how an impressionable young boy falls under the influence of a teacher at the military academy. A frightful
dream, in which he sees himself completely at the mercy of
an evil power, coincides with the teacher's death (FN, 146–
47). The boy thereupon regains self-control. The second report relates how a young girl, who has been put into a
trance by an Italian army officer, is slowly guided back to
health by her boyfriend. Both accounts are interwoven with
the main story which portrays a young girl's destruction at
the hands of Alban, a man who uses his power to break her
will and make her entirely dependent upon him.

Alban expresses his philosophy in a letter in which he
reasons that man must develop his entire potential, including his will to power and those traits which a civilized, weak
society has sought to repress. "All existence is strife and be-
gotten by strife. The strong triumph in a continuously as-
cending climax and increase their power through the van-
quished slaves" (FN, 169–70). His will to power laughs at all
human limitations. Alban hopes to attain his superhuman
strength, apparently his act of self-realization, through the
annihilation of the integrity of others around him. In effect,
he argues that after another self has been absorbed, it not
only becomes a passive mirror of his own intellect but also
increases his intellectual power. And by enhancing his energy he feels closer to the absolute force residing in God.
"Striving for power is striving for the divine, and the degree
of bliss is determined by the intensity of the feeling of
power" (FN, 170). But since God can actually be experienced only as dynamic intellectual energy, He resides
within Alban's mind. Thus any increase in power is justified:
"We enforce the absolute autonomy over the intellectual
wellspring of life" (FN, 170). Alban lives his new morality to
the fullest. Without a trace of remorse he takes over Maria's

mind (FN, 166). When she tries to free herself and marry her old friend, Alban destroys her physical shell also. Her death at the altar is the final victory of his intellect over another body and the moment of triumph for the will as it achieves absolute autonomy over all ethical norms.

If Alban is the intellectual high priest of evil, then Ignaz Denner must be considered his earthly counterpart. Ignaz and his father Dr. Trabacchio, incarnations of evil and satanic compulsion, wander on earth and bring misery to everyone. At times, when Andres's simple faith in God triumphs, the Satanism of the tale seems an inverted form of Christianity. At other times, for instance, in the prison scenes and the slaughter of the child, the story seems to present a glimpse of the world in which Alban's philosophy has taken root. Ignaz delights in his power, never repents, and persists forever (FN, 411–12). Ignaz and his father practice a primitive form of the philosophy of self-enhancement through the assimilation of others. Since they lack identity and spiritual reality (soul), they attempt to achieve selfhood by drinking an elixir brewed from the hearts of their own children. The motif which recurs in *The Serapion Brethren* (S, 528–29) is not only nauseating but also lacks artistic subtlety. It certainly reveals Hoffmann's thinking. Pure evil gains immortality through the sacrifice of innocence. Those who encounter it innocently suffer the most horrible destruction, an ordeal that befalls Andres who loses wife and child, is thrown into prison, and brutally tortured.

Of those compulsively driven to evil, René Cardillac is the most memorable and, judging by the critical attention he has received, one of the most complex characters created by Hoffmann.[10] Many interpretations of "Mademoiselle de Scudéry" have focused on Cardillac as a type of demonic artist. Hoffmann's characterization of other artists lends little credence to this view, however. Indeed, the only artists to whom meaningful parallels can be established are Klingsohr and Heinrich ("The Contest of the Minstrels," ["Der

Kampf der Sänger," 1819]) and the stranger ("Kreisler's Certificate"). The reader who is not familiar with the subtleties of criticism concerning the nature of the artist will more likely be reminded of a fairy-tale figure: the evil dwarf who hordes a treasure and destroys everyone who comes to take it. The almost mythic stature of Cardillac derives from his demonic obsession and the fact that he becomes a visible figure for all the evil that has been cancerously spreading through society. For this reason Hoffmann captures in great detail not only the atmosphere that breeds a succession of crimes but also the fear of a court that condemns as many innocent as guilty persons (S, 653–59).

But while the action revolves around the sustained concealment and final disclosure of Cardillac's crimes, each stage adds importance to Olivier Brusson's fate and the question whether Madeleine de Scudéry, who holds the key to Olivier's release, can save him. The poetess also introduces to the narrative the major theme of unselfish love. Pressured to establish a new court with extraordinary powers to search for the criminals who have robbed and murdered lovers on their way to a rendezvous, the king turns to Madeleine de Scudéry for advice. Though Hoffmann does not state the fact, she replies in the spirit of gallantry and idealized love expressed in her novels. Her reply that "a lover who fears thieves is not worthy of love" has the following consequences: it induces Cardillac to send her his most precious jewels, an act which strains his will power to overcome his compulsion to the breaking point; Olivier's fear that Cardillac will kill the poetess forces him to warn her; the poetess who has looked at the world with great serenity is shocked into awareness of the dark forces in man and is confronted with a heroic love which seems to surpass her imagination.

Contrasted and interwoven with the theme of love is that of compulsion which harms not only those possessed by it but also those confronted with it. Hoffmann introduces the theme when he depicts the fear which seized Paris when first Captain de Sainte Croix and the Marquise de Brinvillier, later la Voisin and others, turn to poisoning their victims out of sheer pleasure after they have killed for profit (S, 654–56). Cardillac's compulsion, in contrast, provides him little joy. Characterized as the unfree man *kat-exochen*, he has become totally enslaved to his obsession for which he holds a malevolent fate responsible (S, 691–92). By giving an explanation which seems rational to Cardillac but superstitious to the reader, Hoffmann accentuates the man's weakness and inability to free himself from his demon. After the first murder he feels peace for the first time in his life. "The specter had disappeared, the voice of Satan was silent. Now I knew the intentions of my evil star; I had to obey or perish!" (S, 694). To be sure, Cardillac does not blindly follow his drive. Fully aware that his demon will force him to seize the jewelry from the poor victim, he struggles, refuses to deliver it, even declines to work for people he respects (S, 664–66). Nevertheless, by consciously designating some to be murdered and others to be robbed, he proclaims himself master over life and death. Since he has no philosophical basis for his action, he fails to achieve Alban's amoral independence. Though Cardillac never regrets his crimes, he has moments of fear for his soul (S, 696). In such a mood and prompted by Scudéry's verse, he decides to give her the jewels. By giving this present to a lady known for her virtue and piety he hopes to find a spokesman for his soul. But his compulsion soon proves the stronger. Raging against himself and Madeleine de Scudéry, he gives in to his demon and finds his own death while attacking a new victim.

The person with whom we identify, whose struggle arouses our pity, and whom we would like to see pardoned, if not legally at least in the spirit of compassion and forgiveness, is Olivier Brusson. From the tale's beginning, he suffers serious misfortunes. Basically good, he is forced into an insoluble dilemma by his conviction that the disclosure of

Cardillac's crimes will destroy Madelon's faith in mankind, by the fact that the administration of justice has been undermined in the state (S, 656, 673, 689), and by his unfailing love for Cardillac's daughter. "Trapped in this labyrinth of crime, torn by love and revulsion, by joy and horror, I was like the condemned soul, beckoned by a beautiful, softly smiling angel but held fast by Satan's burning claws, and the holy angel's loving smile that reflects all the bliss of heaven becomes the most agonizing pain. I thought of flight, even of suicide—but Madelon!" (S, 694–95). Olivier's inner torment certainly equals, perhaps even surpasses, Cardillac's. Every crime committed by Cardillac flings him deeper into a hell of self-accusation and intensifies his suffering. He sees no solution until he puts his fate into the hands of Madeleine de Scudéry. Fully conscious of the disasters wreaked by his silence, he is willing to accept any punishment (S, 681, 684) but, all-too-humanly, hopes for a miracle.

His anguish reaches a climax when he loses the good will of the poetess. Henceforth his actions are dictated solely by the attempt to convince her that he was a victim both innocent and guilty but not a murderer. As the scene with La Regnie shows, she cannot succeed in freeing Olivier as long as she views the world in the light of her own artistic creations (S, 676–79). And she cannot help him after her faith in man has been destroyed: "Never before in her life deceived so bitterly by her emotions, mortally wounded by the hellish power on earth in whose existence she had never believed, Madeleine de Scudéry despaired of all truth" (S, 680). Only after the poetess finally comprehends Olivier's ordeal does she have the power to save him. For through his story she begins to see that while there is room for the high ideals she envisioned, the world contains more evil, human suffering, and ambiguities than she imagined. This awareness is critical for Olivier's rescue since only the full force of her conviction can move the king's heart. By presenting the monarch with a vivid tableau of the events in the form of a work of art that sways him through its poetic truth, she is able to capture his attention and avert disaster for Olivier. The scene and the tale's happy ending for the two lovers seem to contain a promise that there is hope almost beyond hope for the victims of life.

8
The Shattered Self

THE THEMES AND MOTIFS ASSOCIATED WITH the divided self dominate Hoffmann's early novel *The Devil's Elixirs* (1815/16) and stand out in his tale "Gambler's Luck" (1820), written three years before his death. The novel portrays through an extended analysis of the unconscious man's confrontation with the brute force that lies within him. The brief narration depicts a man who has the potential to be good but listens instead to his demons and destroys himself and those around him. Hoffmann masterfully captures in *The Devil's Elixirs* the whole spectrum of man's inner experience in his search for self-realization. Efforts to unravel the plot, to separate action from thought, or to explain rationally the tragic curse can only diminish an appreciation of the novel.[1] It assumes new dimensions, however, if it is viewed as a precursor of the modern psychological novel or a dream sequence in which Hoffmann attempts to portray the hero's psychological state. The reader who becomes conscious that the novel's dreamlike continuity affects his awareness of time gains a deeper appreciation for the character of Medardus.[2]

The action spans a lifetime: from childhood, early years in the monastery, love, intrigue, and crime in the world to the final return to the monastery. The formal arrangement of the chapters and Medardus's own testimony seem to indicate that the novel is autobiographical in character (El, 288). The recollection of childhood and youth is designed to enhance this illusion through a factual and objective narration. Yet, the description is carefully structured around events that point to a past tragedy in the family, foreshadow the future, and reveal the hero's mind. Above all, the story beguiles the unwary reader into adopting the fictitious narrator's subjective point of view, for there is no evidence that Medardus has gained either the self-knowledge or a perspective of the events which could be expected of him at the end of his life. As he is retelling his adventures, he is again overwhelmed by the immediacy of the action, caught in events which he cannot control, and still unable to distinguish between reality and dream. By using a circular narrative structure, Hoffmann seems to suggest that the hero cannot surpass the limitations imposed by his mind.

Since early youth Medardus's behavior is motivated by two antagonistic forces, each of which seeks predominance. He is swayed by the desire to conquer his irrational impulses, transcend his instincts, and become a more civilized person. But he also longs to satisfy his instincts and, free from fear, break every moral code as well as the laws of society. The conflict becomes all the more powerful because Medardus can discern only three choices: He can relinquish the demands of his powerful will and accept in humility the symbol of Saint Rosalia as the affirmation of Christian faith, but he also faces a nightmare of mental anguish should his emotions rebel. He can assert his will to autonomy and negate the dictates of his order as well as his own conscience.

Finally, he can transvaluate the existing moral code, deny all guilt, and safeguard his self in constant defiance of the world. The radical incompatibility of these options leaves Medardus in an insoluble dilemma.

He decides early to join the seminary and thereafter the monastery, ostensibly to atone for his father's sins. Spiritually, however, his decision is based on a resolution in which he rejects all action in favor of a life of contemplation. What beckons is an ordered world oriented toward God, one which adheres to the ethos of self-control (El, 19, 25). His resolve is tested only once by an infatuation for his piano teacher's sister. At a social gathering a friend draws her attention to Medardus whom they observe as he vehemently kisses the girl's gloves. Their derisive laughter drives Medardus back to the seminary where he raves madly all night: "In mad despair I threw myself to the ground—burning tears filled my eyes, I denounced—I cursed the girl—myself—then I prayed and laughed like a madman!" (El, 23). This excessively violent reaction is an early indication of the tensions within his personality. His pride, so greatly hurt by the incident, is restored when he decides in the morning to renounce the world; yet his decision also engenders new conflicts.

Five years after Medardus has taken his vows, his still unsubdued arrogance, vanity, pride, and passion begin to clash with the ascetic ideals of poverty, chastity, and humility.[3] Although the narrator remains silent about these years, the ensuing events justify the conjecture that Medardus has, at least partially, adopted the values of his peers because wild and free enjoyment of his instincts alternates with despair and shame. The initial impulse that propels Medardus out of his retreat appears harmless enough. The Brother who preaches the sermons at the monastery grows too old to fulfill his duties and Medardus is asked to take his place. His first sermon proves to be an enormous success. Medardus feels inspired by heaven—"as if the bright spark of divine

95

inspiration had lit my soul"—and the audience is overwhelmed. Soon the throngs visiting the monastery initiate a
flourishing Medardus cult. And the man who in the beginning delighted only in his ability to arouse his listeners soon
sees himself as charismatic preacher and saint who transcends the world in moments of cosmic consciousness: "I
began to think . . . that my mind had direct contact with
the divine and while on earth could rise above all worldly
concerns; I felt that I was not part of the world and mankind to whom I had been sent to bring consolation and salvation!" (El, 31). He begins to scorn the other monks and as
Savior of mankind demands their adoration. Essentially he
rejects at this point the belief that the self can transcend itself in an ethereal vision, and the beautiful dreams of transcendental faith turn into reveries of influence and power.
His credo "to be oneself is to conquer oneself" has been
transformed into "the powerful will save mankind." A sudden apparition during a sermon leads to the complete col-
lapse of the proud monk. Just as in other tales Hoffmann
employs spectral figures to render the inner atmosphere of
emotions, sensations, and dreams, so here the looming specter, a painter whom Medardus dimly recalls from earliest
childhood, seems to be an artistic device through which
Hoffmann attempts to portray a projection of Medardus's
conscience.[4] The figure of the painter appears whenever
Medardus struggles with his conscience. He first becomes
visible in Medardus's childhood and in the hour of his death
stands at his bed. The painter's fear-inspiring gaze, which
evokes the utmost horror in Medardus whenever he feels
guilty (El, 33, 97), softens to a mild glance when his mind is
at peace (El, 175, 282).

The drives of Medardus are temporarily subdued by his
conscience. A severe, self-imposed penance aimed at subju-
gating his will to power has the desired result: the delight in
moving men through brilliant oratory as well as the attend-
ant feeling of might completely vanish. Fearful and fretful,

Medardus stammers a few more sermons and is finally relieved of his preaching duties. In his hour of despair he is liberated from the coercion of his conscience by taking a sip of the devil's elixir. The elixir, comparable to a modern hallucinatory drug, intermittently frees him and enables him to assert himself fully. Hoffmann obviously delights in creating a mysterious atmosphere surrounding the elixir: Saint Anthony's temptation by Satan; the strange visitors; the enigma of the key (El, 27–29, 34–37). But these conventional elements, frequently found in ghost stories, should neither obscure the elixir's significance nor encourage the explanation that it is the determining factor for Medardus's fall into the abyss of evil. Such an answer is not commensurate with Hoffmann's psychological analysis of his hero.

After analyzing the legend of Saint Anthony's temptation, Medardus reasons that it must be understood as an allegory: perhaps the strange bottle in the cell contains a wondrous old wine which will breathe new life into his tormented body (El, 36). Still, an "inner resistance" prevents him from drinking, and when he finally decides to open the chest, he is frightened away by the painter's terrifying eyes. Only after the Prior and the other monks treat him as if he were mentally incapacitated does he dare to open the bottle. When Medardus drinks the potion, he is freed from his inhibitions and no longer troubled by his conscience. To be sure, his intoxication, the feeling of joy and vitality, his sensuous delight in observing the rising sun, the yearning to advance to the highest position, his arrogance (El, 37–38)—all these traits have not been created but have been liberated by the elixir. He now becomes a strong-willed, powerful, dynamic personality and can follow his passionate drives. He denies the values of Christian morality, for he no longer believes that the wretched are good and will be saved. His new creed reads: the strong and powerful will endure.[5] Indeed, at the height of his exaltation he reaches beyond the limitations of his self and experiences the sensation of intensified consciousness in which he has visions of absolute, amoral power (El, 68, 75).

Henceforth it is impossible to distinguish between real and imagined action in the novel, because reality is but a manifestation of the conscious, semi-conscious, and unconscious patterns of Medardus's experience.[6] The personality of Medardus splits and dissolves when he is unable to separate the desire for self-realization from the yearning for transcendence; his traits and thought assume their own life; even his hallucinations take shape, confront, haunt, and punish him. It is quite possible that the visions of love, incest, and salvation as well as the hallucinations of alter egos, crime, and atonement are projections of Medardus's tortured mind, while he remains immured in his cell. This view would be supported not only by the recurring images of confinement (cell, dark and crowded rooms, prison, coach, dungeon, death cell) but also by the frequent statements which prove Medardus's inability to distinguish between thought and action. He loses all awareness of his own personality—"My own self . . . dissolving into strange figures; I could not perceive, not recognize my own self" (El, 47, 51, 59, 77, 91, 116)—and sees in a nightmare sequence how a part of his self wrests itself out of a stone but remains half-contained in the unformed mass (El, 172). A dark voice proclaims "Thought is action" (El, 175), and Euphemie's ghost tortures him with the outcry, "Your suffering is the thought of outrage and lasts eternally" (El, 222). We also should ask ourselves if Aurelie really confides her love to him as he imagines (El, 40–41), why he feels guilty after Viktorin plunges into the gorge if he has not killed him (El, 48), whether he murders Hermogen (El, 76–77), and what transpires at the Dominicans' tribunal (El, 174, 256). These scenes, in which Hoffmann emphasizes how real the visions are to Medardus and how intensely he lives them, also reveal that, to Medardus, thought *is* action and becoming *is* being. Consequently, imagined evil is punished as severely as a committed crime, a view which explains many seemingly unintelligible events in the novel and sheds light on Medardus's inner conflict when he is confronted with the question of admitting his transgressions.

The stages of Medardus's offenses depict not only the struggle between consciousness and unconsciousness but also the ever widening gulf between pure contemplation and the powerful assertion of the will, that is, between innocence and guilt. Hoffmann captures this conflict in the familiar symbolism of the virgin (Saint Rosalia, Aurelie) and the whore (Euphemie). The strife erupts in seething passion when Medardus has a vision of a girl confiding her love to him in the confessional. He fights the temptation and flogs himself only to become more frenzied. Raging and howling he lies on the steps of the altar—momentarily convinced that it was Saint Rosalia who had stepped out of a painting to declare her love (El, 41). In a calmer mood he feels that he must leave the monastery and seek the fulfillment of his dreams in the world. Once he has really decided to leave, the monastery fades away; just as he has completed his plans to escape, his Prior unexpectedly sends him on a mission to Rome. Hoffmann pictures this entry into the world in the form of a hymn to nature (El, 45), one of the few passages in the novel in which the images of confinement give way to an expression of freedom. The burst of color and light surrounding Medardus reflects his joy in being liberated.

After several days' journey through the mountains he pauses one day at noon. The ensuing events again have the qualities of a dream sequence. Medardus drinks the elixir, encounters Count Viktorin sitting on a cliff on the verge of plunging into a deep gorge, tries to save him, shouts, but the Count vanishes in the ravine (El, 47). Without thought or hesitation Medardus assumes the Count's role. And while one part of his self accuses him of a crime, another part compels him to speak and act instinctively as another personality (El, 48–51).[7] The result of this first distinct split in his personality leads to the sensation of a complete loss of identity: "Capricious chance began to play cruelly with my self and dissolving into strange figures I swam helplessly on an ocean of events which broke over me like raging waves" (El, 59). He is Viktorin, man of the world and adulterer, but he is also Medardus, monk and renegade. As Viktorin he cools his passion in Euphemie's embrace (El, 62); as Medardus he lusts after Aurelie, the personification of his past vision (El, 61).

Two distinct phases are discernible in Medardus's attitude toward Aurelie. At first, she is the object of his sexual desire, an object which he must possess even if it means risking his soul (El, 61). When he meets her again after his initial design has collapsed in a catastrophe, he attempts to establish a sincere relationship. But while the second phase of the courtship is dominated by tender emotions, Medardus is still overwhelmed by paroxysms of passion which again lead to disaster. Initially Medardus like Alban does not hesitate to destroy everyone in his way to achieve his ends. He experiences moments of supreme strength and joy as soon as his will has become autonomous: "Something superhuman had become part of my self and suddenly elevated me to a position which enabled me to see everything in a new light" (El, 68); "Now I had arrived at a point which removed me completely from ordinary human activities" (El, 75); "What are these counts, these barons . . . but helpless, glittering insects whom I shall crush to dust with my fist if they become too annoying" (El, 156); "What could these weaklings do against my might of intellect and spirit?" (El, 168). Confronted with Medardus's dynamic force which repudiates all morality as the code of the weak, all others become helpless victims. Even Euphemie, Aurelie's stepmother, herself an advocate of evil (El, 65–67), succumbs to the demonic power unleashed within him. He rejoices when she reveals her plan for the destruction of Aurelie's brother, because her confidence is but one more indication that he has absolute control of everyone's thought and action. He hatches the monstrous scheme of destroying Euphemie and raping Aurelie at the same moment: "Announcing myself as the evil spirit of revenge, I had to accomplish the monstrosity. Euphemie's destruction was decided and, uniting blazing hate with fervent love, I had to experience a pleasure worthy of the superhuman spirit in me" (El, 75). The first station in Medardus's journey culminates in a scene of horror in which he poisons Euphemie and stabs Aurelie's brother (El, 76). Pursued by the aroused servants Medardus starts to flee, but then turns and proudly proclaims himself the dark spirit of fate. Yet when he looks up he is horrified. It is not he who has raised his voice but a blood-spattered Viktorin who has survived the plunge into the gorge. And away Medardus flees.[8]

His feeling of strength gives way to one of complete helplessness. Medardus drifts along (El, 83), doubting that he can control his destiny (El, 115), feeling isolated even in the presence of others (El, 90), and questioning his very existence (El, 91). Haunted by the vision of the painter (El, 95–97), Medardus flees again and arrives late at night in a secluded forester's home. Against this background Hoffmann most strikingly develops the theme of the loss and search for identity. Medardus is shown to a room, immediately falls asleep and is tortured by a terrifying dream. He sees himself as monk; the figure moves ever closer, finally sits down on his bed and begins to speak: "Now you must come with me . . . let's climb to the roof right under the weathervane which plays a cheerful wedding song because the owl is getting married. There we shall fight with each other and whoever throws the other one down is king and can drink blood" (El, 105). Several indications suggest that Hoffmann designed in the insane monk an ego projection of Medardus which surpasses in conception and presentation the alter ego portraits of the other romantics. It is a concrete figure, a manifestation of Medardus's vision, and a symbol of his innate potential, because it has all those attributes which Medardus hates and yet desires. The fact that the figure incorporates Viktorin's character traits, resembles, and is finally identified with him initially startles the reader (El, 273–76).[9] Still, if we recall how easily Medardus had assumed Viktorin's role in the castle, how he had projected his yearnings and tensions onto him, the association Viktorin—mad monk—alter ego seems to be particularly well suited to reinforce the theme.

The summons of the alter ego recurs four more times: when Medardus is jailed (El, 165), after his release (El, 182–87), on the wedding day (El, 206), and on his deathbed where alter ego and conscience still struggle for his soul (El, 289). The alter ego's chants, especially the blood motif associated with them, testify to the enormous conflict raging within Medardus. The call "Bro-ther . . . o-open up . . . let's go-go to the fo-forest . . . to the forest" (El, 165); the lure to drown in passion, "let's seek the bride" (El, 289); and the challenge to battle until one or the other is destroyed, "Bridegroom, bridegroom! come . . . come to the roof . . . roof . . . there we shall fight with each other and whoever throws the other down is king and can drink blood!" (El, 206; also 105, 182), leave no doubt that Medardus attempts to rid himself of his old identity. When he finally succumbs on the wedding day ("I am king . . . I drink your blood"), he becomes united with his alter ego but collapses in insanity (El, 207). His insanity and the picture of the unshakeable alter ego riding on his back (El, 207) show the utter failure of this primitive attempt. What Medardus has yet to learn from the mirror of his alter ego is the *conscious* recognition of the forces which propel him in life. The exclamations "I could not find myself! I began to have doubt about my identity! I could not see myself!" testify to the inability to achieve a measure of critical insight.

Employing the technique of reciprocal illumination,

Hoffmann introduces the story of the mad monk to mirror the tragedy of Medardus. And as the narrative unfolds, Medardus imitates the monk by becoming insane.[10] The real cause of the monk's insanity is obvious. He had never realized that the prerequisite for true self-realization is a harmonious development of man's total potential. Instead he had given free rein to some emotions to the exclusion of others, had completely negated reason, and finally had become so infatuated with his desires that he lost all control over himself. Nevertheless, he feels innocent. In his view his destruction was caused by an inexplicable fate over which he had absolutely no control (El, 113–14). Likewise Medardus, convinced in his youth of his ability to master fate, now holds demonic powers that are beyond the reach of man responsible for his deeds, and finally sees himself in the cage: "But I had fallen into the hands of an evil, mysterious power that played with me and held me in chains I could not break, so that I, who fancied myself to be free, only moved within a cage in which I was locked forever" (El, 115). This reasoning indicates how far removed Medardus still is from true self insight. Indistinct and contradictory voices speak from within: I am not guilty. My life as a monk was a dream. I am not lost. Still, I am condemned for I have willed evil. The sensation of energy, the pulsating blood, and all action are also illusions.

The feeling of being controlled by an unknown force persists after Medardus leaves the forester's home. Favored by the prince of a small state he is invited to a faro game in the court. While he blindly and mechanically draws cards, he suddenly realizes that he is in danger of completely abdicating his will (El, 129–30). Frightened, he begins to reflect upon his action and concludes: "Any limitation of freedom, even if it is misused, . . . is intolerable" (El, 131). This affirmation of absolute freedom, which precedes the third fateful encounter with Aurelie, points to the sudden rejuvenation of Medardus's powerful will. It is of singular importance in Hoffmann's portrait of Medardus, since it heralds the beginning of a struggle between two conflicting views of man. On the one hand, Medardus still sees life as a constant clash of contending wills; on the other, he struggles earnestly to establish a new relationship with Aurelie, one that is based on respect for others and presupposes an inviolate self.[11] For the first time he doubts that his love can be fulfilled and wonders whether his insatiable yearning can be stilled only in death (El, 153). This basic contradiction is never resolved while Aurelie is alive: outbursts of the demonic wish to possess and annihilate her (El, 154–55, 186) alternate with gentle and profoundly moving scenes (El, 153, 184–85). The struggle continues throughout Medardus's confinement. Indeed it is reflected in the series of nightmares, grotesque apparitions, and the encounter with the alter ego (El, 164–65, 168, 172–73). After the release from prison, which is as mysterious as the arrest, all sinister thoughts briefly vanish. Medardus has extirpated his death wish which threatened him during his confinement, has a vision of salvation, and feels purified by Aurelie's love. But his moderation and self-mastery are deceptive. No sooner is the marriage proposed than discord within him flares up again (El, 188, 204–05). Finally he abandons all noble emotions. Only one thought remains: Aurelie alone can save his soul; she must become his wife. He is driven to annihilate her in order to save his own personality. The blood motif recurs again. He rejects the angelic in favor of the satanic vision and rages in madness. The final scene shows an utter contempt for life and is completely incompatible with the premise of a human dialog. Medardus's attempt fails, since it is based on self-deception. His ruthless will is stronger than the desire to abnegate it in favor of a compassionate relationship.

Medardus regains consciousness in an insane asylum in Italy. Here he finds the wisdom lacking in the world outside. In a scene reminiscent of a comic interlude of clown and tragic hero, he is told why his search must end in disaster. He is unable or unwilling to embrace folly as a guide and abandon reason altogether. Instead he attempts to reconcile his visions with his conscience and, what is even worse, with his conception of reality (El, 213–14). Above all Medardus has not gained the insight which would enable him to recognize his goal (El, 218–19). He still lacks the necessary distance to consider his struggle dispassionately, in short, to comprehend the mysteriously twisted thread of his own self. As Medardus comes to the last stages of his journey, it becomes clear that his road does not lead to self-realization. He confesses at a Capuchin monastery. His punishment and suffering, his visions of purgatory and damnation are as real to him as was the experience of his transgressions (El, 221 ff.). Yet his self-inflicted torture, which apparently seems to insure that henceforth he will remember his pledge, is primarily aimed at breaking his will. His pride and vanity rise to a final grand vision in which he sees himself as holy sinner and saint whose suffering and penance surpassed all transgressions (El, 258). A purifying flame of light consumes his last rebellious thoughts (El, 259–61).

The allegorical dream of the conflict between blood and light points to a solution of the struggle between passion and reason: only after the will has been annihilated shall a purified self rise from the ashes of destruction and embrace the visible and invisible universe. But Medardus who sought realization of his self in the world cannot accept the answer which demands complete self-transcendence. Assailant (his will) and victim (the object of his love) must perish. Thus we are confronted with the picture of Aurelie murdered by the alter ego at the altar after the insane lust to seize and destroy her has raged within Medardus for the last time: "The thought of murder arose in me like a monstrous fiend, like Satan himself! . . . The passion of love, of unbridled lust, raged in me more violently than ever before —'Oh God, oh all you saints! Don't let me become insane, not insane. . . .' Irresistibly one idea seized me: to embrace her with all the passion of my raging lust and then to kill her" (El, 279–81). With Aurelie's death his life's cycle also reaches its end. In his final hour we hear for the last time the alter ego's summons, "Come with me, brother Medardus, we shall look for the bride." But the painter is also with him, indicating that in his visions Medardus has reached an understanding of evil.

The attempt to merge the contradictory forces of humanitarianism and a passionate commitment to life has failed. Once Hoffmann has shown Medardus's failure to guarantee his self by saying yes to life, once he has exposed his hero's inner core of nihilism, no amount of torture and flagellation will civilize him or restore his faith. The interrogations and trials, the hideous and appalling visions of punishment reflect Medardus's suffering and the breaking of his will. And though they indicate that Medardus must atone for what he has willed in his thoughts, they do not mark a fundamental change in the development of his character. Even the brief vision of salvation and the apparent triumph of his conscience on his deathbed cannot change the novel's basic outlook. The narrator's observation, "Then . . . it seemed to me that whatever we generally call dream and imagination could also be the recognition of the secret thread which runs through our life" (El, 8), is meaningful as long as we resist the temptation to see in it merely the affirmation of an inevitable, inexplicable fate or curse that controls Medardus's life.[12] Rather it is an admission of the ultimate futility of human life. Medardus's suffering is symbolic of the anguish of all those who freed themselves, dethroned God, but discovered that their road led to self-crucifixion. The inversion of Christian symbolism from wine to blood, climaxing in the sacrifice of the virgin at the altar, reinforces this view. Archaic instincts, a lust for violence, disorder, and chaos break into an apparently civilized world. The dynamism which propels Medardus beyond the limitations imposed by belief, tradition, environment, and his own mind exhausts itself in dreams, leads to the formation of a permanently split consciousness, and finally to hopeless isolation. The encounters in the search for self-realization prove to be illusory; he ultimately remains caged.

In "Gambler's Luck" Hoffmann uses the image of the cage to characterize a cross section of society. The gambling casinos mirror a world without true love and hope, a world in which men are crushed by their own weakness while they cling to the illusion of mastering their elusive idol. Though the narrative centers on the temptation and subsequent destruction of Chevalier Menars, its power springs from a series of vivid scenes which uncompromisingly state a basic conflict between dignified existence and debasing instincts, between the promise of self-realization and man's ultimate fall. In contrast to other stories, the action in "Gambler's Luck" is clearly designed and the character development is kept to a bare minimum. Here Hoffmann portrays the rapid change of man's fortune when he lacks the strength to resist the lure of his inner demons. Several men unwittingly risk their humaneness, even their lives, when they are confronted by almost identical situations which tempt them to hazard their proverbial good luck. All of them are basically good men of great charm who accept life cheerfully and seem capable of controlling their future.

One, young Baron Siegfried, is saved at the last moment from plunging into the abyss which suddenly opens before him when the story of Chevalier Menars reveals to him the danger in which he finds himself. Another, Colonel Duvernet, risks his soul in the mad desire for vengeance. He loses when death reaps the prize at the moment of victory. Vertua, a professional gambler, refuses a loan to a young man who has just lost a fortune and is thereupon stabbed. Slowly nursed back to life by his wife, he begins to realize that his gambling has killed all human emotions in him (S, 725). He swears never to touch cards again. But when he hears of Menars, he decides to test his luck against the other players' (S, 726). He loses and does not gamble again until his compulsion overwhelms him on his deathbed: "While the priest who had come to bring the consolation of the church to the dying man spoke of spiritual matters, Vertua was lying there, his eyes closed, murmuring *perd—gagne.* He made motions of picking up and turning over cards with hands that were trembling in the throes of death" (S, 731). Sighing *gagne* he dies.

Initially Menars is totally indifferent to gambling. But one day when his small allowance fails to arrive on time, he is reminded that he had once won a considerable sum for another person. He decides to stake twenty Louisdor to become financially independent and, blindly trusting his good luck, plays once more. From this moment Menars has lost control over his actions and henceforth lacks all critical self-perception. His life seems to be ruled completely by the great god chance. Though he gains fortune after fortune, he is so addicted to his new life and the passion for money that he becomes a professional gambler (S, 721). The fame of his unbelievable good luck spreads and finally attracts the old moneylender Vertua who loses to him his huge fortune, including his home.

As unmoved by Vertua's plea for a loan as by his tragic story, Menars is prepared to take over the house. At this moment Vertua's daughter appears. Menars suddenly sees himself in all his ugliness. He falls in love with her and stops gambling. This hyperbolic scene (S, 728) lacks all psychological motivation and can only be explained with reference to the symbolism of the virgin in Hoffmann's work. Confronted with purity at a crucial moment Menars recognizes his weakness and his inner bleakness. He courts and marries Angela who realizes too late that she had always loved Duvernet. Deeply affected by her father's ominous death, she fears the future and has the foreboding that Menars will shed his "mask of an angel," begin to gamble again, and "assume his original satanic shape" (S, 732). Her weakness and desperation only quicken his fall, a fate which parallels that of Vertua. Menars holds the bank again and is despised by everyone for coldly looking on while a young man commits suicide. Accused of fraud he loses his money and returns to his wife. The news of a French colonel's luck tempts him back to the gambling table, where he stakes his wife after he has lost everything else. But death holds the trump: Angela has died.

The gamblers Hoffmann depicts in "Gambler's Luck" do not belong to the category of those who seek to discover a revelation of fate in the mysterious laws of chance (S, 720). Menars and Vertua use their "luck" to enrich themselves and soon fall prey to the most debasing instincts. Initially free men, they become enslaved by their obsession which robs them not only of the control of their own lives but of all love and compassion. When Menars and Duvernet gamble for Angela, their action is not only inhuman but seems to bait a power beyond their control into a struggle in which they are destroyed while hellish laughter echoes from the sky. That they try to play fate with another life remains their most unforgivable sin. In "The Dei of Elba in Paris" ["Der Dei von Elba in Paris. 1815," 1815] Hoffmann clearly states that every such attempt by gamblers, be they Menars or Napoleon, destroys man's goal of self-determination: "The gamble of dark powers for life and freedom shall start again, that hideous gamble which laughs at inner strength and counts only the fortuitous throw that saves us from disaster" (Musik, 632). The gambler Menars, who lacked the strength to control himself, gambled away his freedom, and staked the fate of another person for his profit, symbolizes the shattered self as much as the monk who never found his true self. Their fate and destructive influence on the lives of others conflict sharply with the humanistic stress on ethical norms, the spiritual cultivation of the individual, and the possibility of self-fulfillment through critical self-judgment.

9

The Grand Design and
German Pessimism

HOFFMANN'S WORK WAS BORN OF A crisis in man's self-knowledge. His age was marked by sharply conflicting tendencies. Once the assurance which theoretical knowledge had provided in the preceding century was dissipated, man had to search for a new basis for his existence. Goethe and Schiller had already struggled with the problem. But the ideas set forth in so many of their works that man can liberate himself from the forces threatening his inner freedom only after he has become fully conscious of his motives and that he must courageously accept life and live with his brother became suspect to many writers in the romantic period. Bonaventura in his *Nachtwachen* (1804) rejects the view that the cultural and moral awareness of mankind increases over the centuries. He portrays a world of dancing masks confronted by eternal nothingness. But more than we ever believed, Hoffmann became the sharpest critic of human enslavement through his grand design of the caged man. His work is a constant reminder that, far from having achieved ultimate freedom, man lives in a world of deception and has only begun to walk down the long arduous road to self-realization.

Hoffmann's short stories and tales also presage a trend in the philosophical reasoning of his age. While Hoffmann was neither a philosopher nor a philosophical poet, his judgment of man's existential dilemma almost makes him appear as the novelist of the strong philosophical current of irrationalism and pessimism, which is, notwithstanding appearances to the contrary, an offspring of the great rational philosophical systems of Fichte, Schelling, and Hegel. Despite their differences these philosophers shared several fundamental convictions. They agreed with Kant that the world was an expression of reason and that history revealed a continuous evolution of thought with a concomitant increase in man's self-knowledge. They expanded the transcendental method and freed thought from the Kantian limitations with the result that intellectual life became an independent, continuously developing, and self-governing realm. The emphasis on the spiritual process necessarily transformed the role of the individual and the perception of reality. Though consciousness remains the basis of all experience, the laws of the spiritual sphere (universal idea, absolute spirit, world will) can no longer be acted upon by the individual. Furthermore, since the sphere is self-contained it seems to develop its own momentum and recedes from the immediate perception of the individual. Fichte, Schelling, and Hegel pursued different paths in their search for the essence of spiritual life. "For Fichte, thought is a kind of moral action which subdues the world of lofty ends; for Schelling it is an artistic construction, changing reality within and without us into a living work of art; with Hegel, we see thought spontaneously unfold a process of strict, logical dialectic, embracing all that the world in its evolution has achieved, and reaching its consummation in the thought of thought." [1]

Schelling, whose aesthetic idealism was in spirit closest to the views of the romantic poets, was also the philosopher who inadvertently drew attention to the limitations of transcendental speculations and thus paved the way for a somber appraisal of man's situation. He lectured on the philosophy of art after he had been appointed professor at the University of Jena (1798) and again after he had accepted an appointment in Berlin in 1841. By 1813, Hoffmann had read and studied his book, *Von der Weltseele* (1798). The brothers Schlegel and Novalis were Schelling's friends, and Jacob Burckhardt, Engels, and Kierkegaard attended his lectures in Berlin. In 1800 he published *Der transcendentale Idealismus* in which he stressed the power of creative, aesthetic intuition. This power is at work unconsciously in nature's creations and consciously in man's artistic productions. Therefore Schelling can refer to the objective world as "the original, still unconscious poetry of the Spirit." [2] At the same time the creative intuition becomes the keystone of his system since it demonstrates the process of the ego's self-objectification.

The work of art assumes the most important role in this metaphysical theory because it is the supreme manifestation of the infinite absolute in which consciousness and unconsciousness, the subjective and the objective, the ideal and reality are fused (theory of identity). And man can gain the highest possible knowledge only through aesthetic contemplation. As a result of objections raised to the system of identity, Schelling revaluated and expanded his reasoning in *Philosophie und Religion* (1804) and *Untersuchungen über das Wesen der menschlichen Freiheit* (1809). These works show the desire to find an answer that could be justified by the idealistic system and still satisfy the demands of material existence. He argues that the absolute becomes differentiated on the phenomenal level and introduces the idea of cosmic negation. In negation Schelling sees an elemental force which enables the positive power to assert itself:

"Were it not for the No, the Yes would be without strength." This view provides indeed for a mirror image of the absolute in the form of a "soul" which reflects the nothingness of the phenomenal world.

The precise nature of the relationship between negation and freedom remains ambiguous. Schelling insists that it does not deny the freedom of the individual. Because the human spirit reflects creative unity which rests in God, the eternal conflict between light and darkness, assumed to be within Him, would also be evident in man. The human personality, in a steady process of becoming and of forever struggling to realize itself, must seek to overcome its unconscious impulses and defeat its selfish will. But since man could also either follow his drives or lose his struggle for self-realization, his existence is much more endangered than Schelling initially was willing to admit. His later view does not deny the threat to man arising from the irrational, powerful forces within him.

Schelling's recognition reflects a growing interest in man's "double personality," in the unconscious, and subsequently in man's corporeal nature, found in the works of the German romantics. Hoffmann's keen interest in dreams, trancelike and ecstatic states is shared by contemporary writers and philosophers, notably Gotthilf Heinrich Schubert whose *Ansichten von der Nachtseite der Naturwissenschaft* (1808) and *Symbolik des Traumes* (1814) Hoffmann had read. Schubert did not intend to question the generalizations of the transcendental method. Yet his publications greatly enhanced the appreciation of the non-rational aspects of life. A systematic attack against the very foundation of idealism came from Friedrich Bouterwek, who was Schopenhauer's teacher at Göttingen. He reasoned in his *Apodiktik* (1799) that transcendental philosophy cannot affirm anything with absolute knowledge about either the thing-in-itself or the object. Man possesses only an incomplete knowledge of the objective world which he gains through the consciousness of willing. The will is the primary force that motivates the individual. By willing, the individual also recognizes the object because it resists the will. Thus force and resistance form the basis for our knowledge of the self and reality.

The increasing perception of the irrational among the romantic writers and the philosophical recognition that consciousness originated from the assertion of the will were cast into a metaphysical system by Arthur Schopenhauer.[3] In his work Hoffmann's artistic creations received their philosophical justification. The powerful assertion of the will by Alban and Medardus, their laughter at the view that history revealed a continuous growth in man's consciousness, and their rejection of the idea of a harmonious fulfillment of man's potential anticipate Schopenhauer's transformation of old values. *Die Welt als Wille und Vorstellung* (1819) constitutes the metaphysical foundation of pessimism. The movements of history can no longer be explained rationally. The world does not indicate a progress in man's spiritual achievement. Philosophy is incapable of attaining ultimate truth but expresses the ideas of a particular time and period. And life itself is propelled by the dynamic force of the will which overpowers the individual's intellect and extends its influence over the whole range of man's experience. Schopenhauer sees the essence of life in this will to live which objectifies itself in eros and forever begets itself. Since each momentary achievement leads to new desires, the will is never satisfied. Thus human existence is confined to an eternal struggle for self-assertion and failure, a process of becoming and disintegration, of suffering and ultimate nothingness which can only be alleviated by compassion and aesthetic experiences or broken by the complete negation of the will, the rejection of life. Consequently man should free himself from his illusions and say yes to suffering and death.

The philosopher, distrusting the noble aspirations of idealism, bitterly feels the limitations of life. The faith that man can be fundamentally improved has been lost. Man, society, and history seem to hold no promise of change for the better. Thematically, Hoffmann's work settles an account with the past and also points to the literature of our time which voices his concern. Hoffmann captures the spirit of man's suffering, his feeling of apprehension and *Weltangst* in the picture of the defenseless persons who are attacked by unconscious forces from within and by powerful, evil wills from without. Certainly Hoffmann's grand design in which he identifies the feeling of dread that encompasses being and becoming with man's existence, and the image of the cage with the structure of the world reveals his consummate skill in portraying the disintegration of the individual in a world of uncontrolled forces. Fleeing from inner demons, hiding from the fear-inspiring eye of evil, and tortured by visions of an infernal world, many of Hoffmann's characters rush through a labyrinth of streets or lose themselves in a forest of darkness. Hoffmann's grand design raises serious doubts concerning man's ability to master his destiny but also presents the reader with the challenge to free himself from the limitations of his life and transcend his caged existence.

To bring man's suffering into clear focus, Hoffmann employs the imagery of marionettes, puppets, mechanical dolls, the cipher of an evil fate or curse, the motifs of drinking blood, of human sacrifice at the altar, and the artistic structure of the infernal fairy tale. The dynamic relationship between apocalyptic symbolism (almandine, soul, temple, Atlantis) and infernal symbolism (imagery of blood, cannibalism, cage, shattered self) illuminates the tension between yearning for self-transcendence and the brutal assertion of the will. Stylistically, the inner and outer tensions of man are reflected in an artistic pattern of increasing momentum which is sustained by contrasts, sudden clashes, unexpected actions, conflicting voices, and the recurrent, alternating movement between detail and concrete universal.

Each age, we are told, rewrites the literature of the past in its own image. E.T.A. Hoffmann, as he appears in my appraisal, seems to reflect modern distinctions and preferences. Yet students of Hoffmann and German romanticism know that the themes and problems discussed first became of critical interest in the beginning of the nineteenth century. As long as an optimistic confidence in the world and the social order prevailed, Hoffmann had little chance to attain widespread recognition among critics. Perhaps he seems very modern to us only because his deep concern with the quest for self-realization is as timeless as his account of the internal tensions and external conflicts besetting man. His view of the world lacks all shallow optimism. Atlantis beckons, but it seems to be the desperate cry of a tormented artist who knows that the infernal cage exists here and now. Even the dreams of fairyland prove to be illusions because the beautiful glitter cannot hide the anguish of its people. And while lonely artists battle a soulless, dehumanized world, Hoffmann seriously questions the mission of art and the artist in *Nutcracker and the King of Mice*. Not surprisingly, the themes of self-assertion and negation, love and compulsion, angelic and satanic vision, freedom and enslavement and the motifs of the cage, the consuming circle, and the shattered self form the basic constellation of his design.

Though many struggle almost beyond endurance for self-realization, they discover that their road leads into a confining circle which they can transcend only in dreams or death. Kreisler's life not only reflects the tragedy of other artists who confront an uncomprehending public, see the rise of pseudo-artists like Murr and Milo, and tend to lose themselves in beautiful, transcendental visions but also symbolizes the anguish of man in general. And if Kreisler's heroic struggle and Tyss's victory show us the potential in man, then the journeys of Fröbom and Medardus into the interior reveal an important aspect of man's inner nature. Hoffmann presents a picture of man in the process of development whose struggle for self-knowledge is played out against the background of a gigantic dance of masks and shattered selves who are convinced that an "unknown, sinister fate" has bound them to the wheel. While some risk their souls to free themselves and others follow their compulsion, while true heroes struggle in tragic isolation and unsung victims of evil are destroyed in an incomprehensible world, the modern anti-hero has already entered the stage. Caged, torn in inner conflict, isolated, schizophrenic, absurd, and utterly fantastic, he tumbles from cell to cell or ends his life in a hallucinatory nightmare.

notes

References to standard works and studies of previous decades on Hoff-mann have been omitted since the cited Hoffmann editions have excel-lent selected bibliographies. Exhaustive bibliographical references are found in: *Goedekes Grundriss* 14: 352–490, 1008–14 (Kron & Kanzog); Jürgen Voerster, *160 Jahre E.T.A. Hoffmann-Forschung 1805–1965: Eine Bibliographie mit Inhaltserfassung und Erläuterungen.* Stuttgart: Eggert, 1967; and in the *Mitteilungen der E.T.A. Hoffmann Gesellschaft* (MHG):

Klaus Kanzog, "Grundzüge der E.T.A.-Hoffmann-Forschung seit 1945," *MHG* 9 (1962): 1–30;

———, "E.T.A. Hoffmann-Literatur 1962–1965. Eine Bibliographie," *MHG* 12 (1966): 33–38;

———, "E.T.A. Hoffmann-Literatur 1966–1969. Eine Bibliographie," *MHG* 16 (1970): 28–40.

Chapter I

1. Ludwig Börne, *Gesammelte Schriften*, ed. Alfred Klaar (Leipzig, 1899), 3: 105–109, 185–90.

2. Charles E. Passage, *The Russian Hoffmannists* (The Hague, 1963), p. 238.

Chapter II

1. Hermann August Korff, *Geist der Goethezeit* (Leipzig, 1964), 4: 543.

2. See Arthur Gloor, *E.T.A. Hoffmann. Der Dichter der entwurzelten Geistigkeit* (Zurich, 1947); Jean-F.-A. Ricci, *E.T.A. Hoffmann. L'homme et l'oeuvre* (Paris, 1947); Harvey W. Hewett-Thayer, *Hoffmann: Author of the Tales* (Princeton, 1948); Regine Jebsen, "Kunstanschauung und Wirklichkeitsbezug bei E.T.A. Hoffmann" (Ph.D. diss., Kiel, 1952); Fritz Martini, "Die Märchendichtung E.T.A. Hoffmanns," *Deutschunterricht* 7, No. 2 (1955): 56–78; Wolfgang Kayser, *Das Groteske. Seine Gestaltung in Malerei und Dichtung* (Oldenburg, 1957); Hans Mayer, "Die Wirklichkeit E.T.A. Hoffmanns," in his *Von Lessing bis Thomas Mann* (Pfullingen, 1959), pp. 198–246; Walter Müller-Seidel, "Nachwort," FN, 749–70 and "Nachwort," El, 667–89; Marianne Thalmann, *Das Märchen und die Moderne* (Stuttgart, 1961), pp. 78–103; Friedrich Giselher Tretter, "Die Frage nach der Wirklichkeit bei E.T.A. Hoffmann" (Ph.D. diss., Munich, 1961); Hans-Georg Werner, *E.T.A. Hoffmann. Darstellung und Deutung der Wirklichkeit im dichterischen Werk* (Weimar, 1962); Robert Mühlher, "Die Einheit der Künste und das Orphische bei E.T.A. Hoffmann," in *Stoffe, Formen, Strukturen*, ed. Albert Fuchs and Helmut Motekat (Munich, 1962), pp. 345–60; Robert Mühlher, "E.T.A. Hoffmann und das Spätbarock," *Jahrbuch d. Wiener Goethe-Vereins* 67 (1963): 139–52; Robert Mühlher, "Ernst Theodor Amadeus Hoffmann. Beiträge zu einer Motiv-Interpretation," *Literaturwiss. Jahrbuch d. Görres-Ges.*, N.F. 4 (1963): 55–72; Robert Mollenauer, "The Three Periods of E.T.A. Hoffmann's Romanticism: An Attempt at a Definition," *Studies in Romanticism* 2 (1963): 213–43; Ronald Taylor, *Hoffmann* (London, 1963); Kenneth Negus, *E.T.A. Hoffmann's Other World* (Philadelphia, 1965); Thomas Cramer, *Das Groteske bei E.T.A. Hoffmann* (Munich, 1966); Lothar Köhn, *Vieldeutige Welt* (Tübingen, 1966); Volkmar Sander, "Realität und Bewusstsein bei E.T.A. Hoffmann," in *Studies in Germanic Languages and Literature*. Presented to Professor E.A.G. Rose, ed. Robert A. Fowkes and Volkmar Sander (New York, Reutlingen, 1967), pp. 115–26; Wulf Segebrecht, *Autobiographie und Dichtung. Eine Studie zum Werk E.T.A. Hoffmanns* (Stuttgart, 1967); Wulf Segebrecht, "E.T.A. Hoffmanns Auffassung vom Richteramt und vom Dichterberuf. Mit unbekannten Zeugnissen aus Hoffmanns juristischer Tätigkeit," *Jahrbuch d. dt. Schillerges.* 11 (1967): 62–138; Marianne Thalmann, *The Literary Sign Language of German Romanticism*, trans. Harold A. Basilius (Detroit, 1972); René Wellek, "Why Read E.T.A. Hoffmann?," *Midway* 8 (1967): 49–56; Karin Cramer, "Die Fragwürdigkeit der menschlichen Identität," *MHG* 14 (1968): 31–38; Horst S. Daemmrich, "Zu E.T.A. Hoffmanns Bestimmung ästhetischer Fragen," *Weimarer Beiträge* 14 (1968): 640–63.

3. Hans Mayer, p. 211, notes that reality becomes an integral yet distinctly discernible part of the works: "Man erkennt: das Gegeneinander der beiden Welten in Hoffmanns poetischem Werk dient letztlich doch

nicht, wie bei den anderen Romantikern, einer Entwesung der Wirklichkeit. . . . Das Gegeneinander der beiden Welten, der realen und der mythischen, erscheint als Ausdruck ungelöster deutscher Gesellschaftsverhältnisse." Hans-Georg Werner, however, rejects this conclusion: "In den Dichtungen E.T.A. Hoffmanns dienten die phantastischen Elemente jedoch der . . . künstlerischen Absicht, die Wirklichkeit zu entwerten und sie auf eine übersinnliche Welt zu beziehen" (p. 192; cf. also pp. 44, 110, 118). See also Ricci, pp. 100 ff.; Peter Bruning, "E.T.A. Hoffmann and the Philistine," *German Quarterly* 28 (1955): 111–21; Klaus F. Köpp, "Realismus in E.T.A. Hoffmanns Erzählung 'Prinzessin Brambilla,'" *Weimarer Beiträge* 12 (1966): 51–80.

4. See my "Wirklichkeit als Form: Ein Aspekt Hoffmannscher Erzählkunst," *Colloquia Germanica* 4 (1970): 36–45.

5. Thalmann, *Sign Language*, p. 55: "From aesthetic tradition he derives a scene that is effective because of his routine use of cryptology. He sets up an illusory stage from everything available, so to speak, in the warehouse. One could almost say that he pastes the moon on the sky, pushes the clouds aside, stretches out the rainbow, and turns the fountains on." See also pp. 65–66, 72–73.

6. Hans-Georg Werner, p. 44, and Walter Jost, *Von Ludwig Tieck zu E.T.A. Hoffmann. Studien zur Entwicklungsgeschichte des romantischen Subjektivismus* (Frankfurt, 1921), p. 43.

7. Thomas Cramer, p. 56 ff.; Ingrid Strohschneider-Kohrs, *Die romantische Ironie in Theorie und Gestaltung* (Tübingen, 1960), pp. 354–55.

8. Especially noteworthy are the studies by Kenneth Negus, Robert Mühlher, and Marianne Thalmann. See Kenneth Negus, "Thematic Structures in Three Major Works of E.T.A. Hoffmann" (Ph.D. diss., Princeton, 1957); Robert Mühlher, "Liebestod und Spiegelmythe in Hoffmanns Märchen 'Der goldne Topf,'" in his *Dichtung der Krise* (Vienna, 1951), pp. 43–95; Mühlher, *Literaturwis. Jahrbuch d. Görres Ges*, N.F. 4 (1963): 55–72; Thalmann, *Sign Language*; see also Aniela Jaffé, "Bilder und Symbole aus E.T.A. Hoffmanns Märchen 'Der goldne Topf,'" in Carl G. Jung, *Gestaltungen des Unbewussten* (Zurich, 1950), pp. 239–616; Norman H. Binger, "Verbal Irony in the Works of E.T.A. Hoffmann" (Ph.D. diss., Ohio State University, 1942); Hubert Ohl, "Der reisende Enthusiast, Studien zur Haltung des Erzählers in den 'Fantasiestücken' E.T.A. Hoffmanns" (Ph.D. diss., Frankfurt, 1955); Christel Schütz, "Studien zur Erzählkunst E.T.A. Hoffmanns" (Ph.D. diss., Göttingen, 1955); August Langen, in *Deutsche Philologie im Aufriss*, 2d. ed. (Berlin, 1957), I, col., 1252–57; Klaus Rockenbach, "Bauformen romantischer Kunstmärchen. Eine Studie zur epischen Integration des Wunderbaren bei E.T.A. Hoffmann" (Ph.D. diss., Bonn, 1957), Wolfgang Preisendanz, *Humor als dichterische Einbildungskraft. Studien zur Erzählkunst des poetischen Realismus* (Munich, 1963); Preisendanz, "Eines matt ge-

schliffnen Spiegels dunkler Widerschein," in *Festschrift für Jost Trier zum 70. Geburtstag*, ed. William Foerste und Karl Heinz Borck (Cologne, 1964), pp. 411–29; Helmut Müller, *Untersuchungen zum Problem der Formelhaftigkeit bei E.T.A. Hoffmann* (Bern, 1964); Klaus Kanzog's suggestion, "Anstelle des Begriffs 'Novelle' sollte für Hoffmann nur der Begriff *Erzählung* angewandt werden . . ." ("Grundzüge," p. 8), merits serious consideration.

9. Victor Terras, "E.T.A. Hoffmanns polyphonische Erzählkunst," *German Quarterly* 39 (1966): 549–69.

10. Köhn, pp. 50–52, 95–96; Köhn also tries to explore the similarities between Hoffmann's style and musical forms, an approach perfected by Steven Paul Scher, *Verbal Music in German Literature* (New Haven, 1968); Segebrecht, *Autobiographie*, pp. 8 ff., 40 ff., 61, 128.

11. See Mario Praz, *The Romantic Agony* (New York, 1956); Werner Kohlschmidt, "Nihilismus der Romantik," in *Form und Innerlichkeit. Beiträge zur Geschichte und Wirkung der deutschen Klassik und Romantik* (Bern, 1955), pp. 157–76; Franz Schultz, *Klassik und Romantik*, 3d. ed. (Stuttgart, 1959), 2: 48–49, 291, 320–21, 402; Morse Peckham, *Beyond the Tragic Vision. The Quest for Identity in the Nineteenth Century* (New York, 1962), pp. 209–10; Morse Peckham, *Man's Rage for Chaos. Biology, Behavior, and the Arts* (Philadelphia, 1965); Karl S. Guthke, "Der Mythos des Bösen in der westeuropäischen Romantik," *Colloquia Germanica* 2 (1968): 1–36; Sander, pp. 115–26; Theodor Ziolkowski, "Das Nachleben der Romantik in der modernen deutschen Literatur. Methodologische Überlegungen," in Wolfgang Paulsen, ed., *Das Nachleben der Romantik in der modernen deutschen Literatur* (Heidelberg, 1969), pp. 15–31; Günter Wöllner, *E.T.A. Hoffmann und Franz Kafka. Von der "fortgeführten Metapher" zum "sinnlichen Paradox,"* Sprache und Dichtung, vol. 20 (Bern, 1971).

Chapter III

1. The view that Gluck is insane, most pronounced in the studies by Korff, *Geist der Goethezeit*, 4: 550, and Joachim Rosteutscher, *Das ästhetische Idol im Werke von Winckelmann, Novalis, Hoffmann, Goethe, George und Rilke* (Bern, 1956), p. 163, was questioned by Mayer, pp. 198–246 and Köhn, pp. 35–43.

2. See Jebsen, "Kunstanschauung," and Daemmrich, "Bestimmung ästhetischer Fragen."

3. Cf. W, 1: 101, 137, 223; 4: 108; 6: 48, 58; 12: 207; 13: 38, 41; 14: 9, 41.

4. FN, 27 f., 36–41; Murr, 382. It would be misleading to equate completely Kreisler's view with Hoffmann's since he must have been aware that his picture did not correspond to the actual situation. But deeply troubled by a problem which did (and still does) need reform, he overstated his case.

5. See especially Hoffmann's discussion in "Der vollkommene Maschinist" (1814), "Nachricht von den neuesten Schicksalen des Hundes Berganza" (1814), and "Seltsame Leiden eines Theater-Direktors" (1819).

6. Cf. "She only mirrors our highest ideal which is reflected in life in the figure of a stranger" (S, 74). See also W, 9: 242–43 and Hoffmann's explanation of Klärchen's role in Goethe's *Egmont* (W, 13: 147). Hoffmann's choice of the untouched woman has religious overtones (the cult of the Virgin Mary in "Die Jesuiterkirche in G." and *Die Elixiere des Teufels*) but also reflects his personal tragedy with Julia.

7. Compare in this connection: 1. Hoffmann's interpretation of Don Juan who hopes to still his yearning through passion; 2. The contrast between pure, pious love (Wolfframb) and sensuous lust (Heinrich) in "Der Kampf der Sänger" (1811, publ. 1819). In this story Hoffmann identifies outright sensuous desires with evil. Wolfframb's victory over Nasias is made possible through his song inspired by his ideal (S, 274–316); 3. "Die Fermate" (1815): "Happy the composer who never in his life sees *her* again who inspired with mystic power his creative imagination . . . She assumes shape as a beautiful, heavenly tone which lives forever in eternal beauty and youth and inspires melodies which incorporate her again and again (S, 74); 4. The statement in "Meister Martin der Küfner" (1819), (S, 462).

8. See esp. the letter to Speyer, May 1, 1820, *E.T.A. Hoffmann im persönlichen und brieflichen Verkehr. Sein Briefwechsel und die Erinnerungen seiner Bekannten*, ed. Hans von Müller (Berlin, 1912), 2: 405; hereafter cited as Müller-Briefe, and John D. Cronin, "Die Gestalt der Geliebten in den poetischen Werken E.T.A. Hoffmanns," (Ph.D. diss., Bonn, 1967).

9. E.T.A. Hoffmann, *Schriften zur Musik. Nachlese*, ed. Friedrich Schnapp (Darmstadt, 1966), 651–52; hereafter cited as Musik.

10. Hoffmann shares this conception of nature with many of his contemporaries. See Georg Ellinger's introduction to Hoffmann's works (W, I: cxxi). Ellinger traces the parallels between Schubert's, Schelling's, and Hoffmann's view of nature. However, one should not forget the many differences and also remember that Schiller developed already similar ideas which influenced many writers at the time. Schiller's distinction between "wahrer, wirklicher, reiner und roher Natur" seems to be of particular relevance. Cf. Friedrich Schiller, "Über naive und sentimentalische Dichtung," in *Sämtliche Werke. Säkular-Ausgabe*, ed. Eduard v.d. Hellen, 16 vols. (Stuttgart, 1904–1905), 12: 233 ff. See also Otto Friedrich Bollnow, "Der 'Goldne Topf' und die Naturphilosophie der Romantik," in Bollnow, *Unruhe und Geborgenheit im Weltbild neuerer Dichter* (Stuttgart, 1953), 207–26.

11. See W, 1: 56; W, 5: 117; W, 12: 144, and Müller-Briefe, 1: 200: ". . . a colorful world of magic appearance glimmers and flashes around me—it seems as if something great must happen soon—as if a creative work is to arise from the chaos!" Cf. with W, 1: 308 and W, 3: 114.

12. W, 1: 309; W, 5: 94, 117–20; Müller-Briefe, 2: 55 ff., 357: "schlafend komponieren und die Komposition sofort aufgeführt hören." Visions may inspire the artist to create; they are not identical with the creative process. Since the vision itself has its roots in an experience of the actual world, it should not be viewed as totally divorced from reality, even though no such relationship is discernible during the trance.

13. See W, 1: 57, 134, 309–10; W, 3: 111, 113; W, 8: 33; W, 2: 144.

14. W, 1: 134. Hoffmann discusses these ideas in great detail in "Des Vetters Eckfenster" (1822); see esp. W, 12: 145–47, 154–56.

15. See W, 6: 147: "To perceive the specific characteristics of the world around us requires a special sensibility and a penetrating glance. But such perception is not enough. The artist with a truly creative imagination first analyzes, as it were, the colorful diverse impressions of the world in a laboratory and only then do the figures who encompass the whole range of human life come forth like a precipitate of a chemical process."

16. W, 5: 272; see also *E.T.A. Hoffmanns Briefwechsel*, ed. Friedrich Schnapp. 3 vols. (Darmstadt, 1967–1969), 1: 194; hereafter cited as Schnapp-Briefe; W, 1: 310; and W, 1: 301: "In short, the artist must be truly inspired in order to really move us; but the art to compose effectively requires that he retain what he experienced unconsciously in a state of ecstasy with high intelligence in the hieroglyphics of sounds (the notes)."

17. W, 1: 50; W, 4: 61–62; W, 13: 43.

18. See W, 12: 142 f., 216.

Chapter IV

1. See FN, 25–32, 284–297; Murr, 340 ff., 355 ff., 542 ff.

2. Cf. FN, 295; Murr, 414–16, 430, 544.

3. Korff's pointed but onesided evaluation (Korff, 4: 545 ff.) of Kreisler's creative process has been taken up again by Christa Karoli, *Ideal und Krise enthusiastischen Künstlertums in der deutschen Romantik* (Bonn, 1968), pp. 100–73.

4. Scholars have differed widely in their appraisal of the novel; cf. Hans Heinrich Borchert, *Der Roman der Goethezeit* (Stuttgart, 1949), pp. 503–22; Bernhard Heimrich, *Fiktion und Fiktionsironie in Theorie und Dichtung der deutschen Romantik* (Tübingen, 1968), pp. 110–18; Korff, 4: 582–91; Herbert Singer, "E.T.A. Hoffmann. Kater Murr," in *Der deutsche Roman vom Barock bis zur Gegenwart*, ed. Benno v. Wiese (Düsseldorf, 1963), 1: 301–28; Taylor, pp. 26 ff.; Heinz Loevenich, "Einheit und Symbolik des Kater Murr. Zur Einführung in Hoffmanns Roman," *Deutschunterricht*, 16, No. 2 (1964): 72–86; Benno von Wiese, *Von Lessing bis Grabbe. Studien zur deutschen Klassik und Romantik* (Düssel-

dorf, 1968), pp. 248–67; Robert Rosen, *E.T.A. Hoffmanns "Kater Murr"; Aufbauformen und Erzählsituationen* (Bonn, 1970).

5. Murr, 324, 362–67, 417, 453–55, 597–99. Cf. Herman Meyer, *Das Zitat in der Erzählkunst* (Stuttgart, 1961), pp. 114–34.

6. FN, 325–26; Murr, 355, 368, 513, 653. Korff, 4: 552–54 interprets the conflict as one between a too rational artistic approach and irrational boundless visions. What he fails to see is Kreisler's faith in art and his search for new forms. Cf. also Karoli, pp. 102, 109, 112.

7. FN, 295; see also Murr, 430, 518, and the tragedy of Leonard Ettlinger who looks as though he were Kreisler's brother, Murr, 428–29. Hoffmann pictures at length the conflict between primitive, demonic incantations and religious music in "Der Kampf der Sänger," S, 274–316.

8. See also Murr, 653: ". . . is it wrong to rise on seraphic wings of song above everything mundane and strive lovingly and piously for the divine?" Hoffmann's reviews of musical compositions show that he had a decided preference for the old masters.

Chapter V

1. See Sigmund Freud, *Das Unheimliche* (Frankfurt, 1963), pp. 53 ff. Cf. Köhn, pp. 92 ff.; Ernst F. Hoffmann, "Zu E.T.A. Hoffmanns 'Sandmann,' " *Monatshefte* 54 (1962): 244–52; S. S. Prawer, "Hoffmann's Uncanny Guest: A Reading of *Der Sandmann*," *German Life & Letters* 18 (1965): 297–308.

2. Cf. FN, 357; in effect he has lost his sense of selfhood as Buber and Jung perceived it; see Martin Buber, "Urdistanz und Beziehung," *Werke* (Munich, 1962), 1: 411–23, and Carl G. Jung, "Über Mandalasymbolik," in *Gestaltungen des Unbewussten* (Zurich, 1950), pp. 192–93.

3. Interpretations have primarily focused on the theme of art. See esp. Segebrecht, *Autobiographie*, p. 134, and Benno v. Wiese, "Rat Krespel," in *Die deutsche Novelle von Goethe bis Kafka*, 2 vols. (Düsseldorf, 1960/1962), 2: 87–103.

4. The view expressed by Walther Rehm, *Der Todesgedanke in der deutschen Dichtung vom Mittelalter bis zur Romantik* (Halle, 1928), p. 446, that Hoffmann portrayed death in his works only as "Liebestod" cannot be substantiated. See below my interpretation of "Die Bergwerke zu Falun," but also Wulf Segebrecht, "Hoffmanns Todesdarstellungen," *MHG* 12 (1966): 11–19, who argues: "Der Tod behält nicht das letzte Wort, nicht in Hoffmanns Geschichtsauffassung und noch weniger in seiner Dichtung; denn die Darstellungen der Todessehnsucht selbst richten sich, weil sie sich der Kunst verpflichtet wissen, auf das Leben. Der Tod ist bei Hoffmann Thema, nicht Ziel der Dichtung" (p. 10).

5. See FN, 41–49, 285–96; Musik, 884–85. For a general discussion of the

art-as-cult development, see R. P. Blackmur, "The Artist as Hero," in *The Lion and the Honeycomb. Essays in Solicitude and Critique* (New York, 1955), pp. 43–50; and Maurice Beebe, "Art as Religion," in *Ivory Towers and Sacred Founts* (New York, 1964), pp. 114–71.

Chapter VI

1. Martini, "Märchendichtungen," pp. 56–78, questioned this view.

2. Müller-Seidel, "Meister Floh," SW, 899–913; William McClain, "E.T.A. Hoffmann as Psychological Realist. A Study of 'Meister Floh,'" *Monatshefte* 47 (1955): 65–80.

3. Cf. the striking similarity to Schiller's criticism of man who is incapable of developing his potential, in Friedrich Schiller, *Über die ästhetische Erziehung des Menschen in einer Reihe von Briefen* (1793–1794).

4. Interpretations have taken two different directions. Walter Harich, *E.T.A. Hoffmann. Das Leben eines Künstlers*, 2 vols. (Berlin, 1920), 2: 108, sees in the fairy tale a simple allegory and restricts the fight to a struggle between imagination and gloomy education. Urs Orland von Planta, *E.T.A. Hoffmanns Märchen "Das fremde Kind"* (Bern, 1958), considers the work as one of Hoffmann's greatest masterpieces and interprets the clash as symbolic confrontation between romanticism and enlightenment, soul and reason, naturalness and decadence; see p. 68: "Wie vielmehr der Magister Tinte nicht einfach einen kleinlichen Schulmeister und Kinderplager, sondern das Denken überhaupt, das die bunte Welt zur Einöde macht, ja das böse, lebensfeindliche, vernichtende Prinzip an sich vorstellt, so ist das fremde Kind nicht nur ein Sinnbild des reichen, kindlichen Innenlebens, sondern die Seele überhaupt, das Allbelebende, das gute Prinzip in Hoffmanns zweigeteilter Welt, das volle goldene Glück und Leben selbst, das Hoffmann von der Geisteskultur und Aufklärung bedroht sieht."

5. S, 254: "According to these [observations] the fairy tale demands a quiet flow of narration and a certain naiveté of presentation which capture the reader's soul like tender improvised music without clamor and noise."

6. See SW, 14, 15, 48–49, 62–64, 69, 71, 87–88, 95–96.

7. W, 1: 133–34; see also W, 1: 27; W, 5: 74; W, 10: 259–62; and concerning music W, 6: 152: "The sensitivity to the highest and holiest, the spirit that breathes life into nature, is audible in music. Therefore music, in expressing the abundance of life, praises God. The essence of music is a religious cult and its origin to be found in religion alone."

8. Cf. SW, 93.

9. The reader is reminded that as jurist Hoffmann fought valiantly the disregard for the law. See his letter to Hippel, June 24, 1820, Schnapp-

Briefe, 2: 263; SW, 835–39; Wulf Segebrecht, "E.T.A. Hoffmanns Auffassung vom Richteramt," pp. 62–138.

10. Cf. Robert Mühlher, "Prinzessin Brambilla. Ein Beitrag zum Verständnis der Dichtung," *MHG* 5 (1968): 5–24; Werner, p. 153 f. stresses the pessimistic undercurrents, whereas Martini, p. 74, assumes that Giglio Fava and Giacinta Svardi play roles in a dream play and return purified to earth.

11. SW, 689, 720 f., 736 ff., 739–40, 742–44, 751 ff.

12. Cf. Jung's explanation of symbols of self-realization in "Zur Empirie des Individuationsprozesses," and "Über Mandalasymbolik," in *Gestaltungen des Unbewussten*, pp. 95–186, 207.

Chapter VII

1. Marianne Thalmann has markedly changed the emphasis in her assessment of these stylistic features. While she viewed them negatively in *Der Trivialroman des 18. Jahrhunderts und der romantische Roman* (Berlin, 1923), pp. 174 ff., 233, 322 f., she praises Hoffmann's "sovereignty over reality" and "manneristic visions" in *Sign Language*, pp. 51–56, 72. Cf. also Thalmann, *Romantik und Manierismus* (Stuttgart, 1963).

2. The trend is analyzed in detail by Odo Marquard, "Zur Bedeutung der Theorie des Unbewussten für eine Theorie der nicht mehr schönen Kunst," in H. R. Jauss, ed., *Die nicht mehr schönen Künste. Grenzphänomene des Ästhetischen* (Munich, 1968), pp. 375–92.

3. Cf. Dietrich Kreplin, "Das Automaten-Motiv bei E.T.A. Hoffmann," (Ph.D. diss., Bonn, 1957), and Dieter Müller, "Zeit der Automate. Zum Automatenproblem bei Hoffmann," *MHG* 12 (1966): 1–10.

4. Klaus J. Heinisch, "E.T.A. Hoffmann. Das Majorat," in Heinisch, *Deutsche Romantik. Interpretationen* (Paderborn, 1966), pp. 171–74. While evidence for such a view can be found in statements throughout Hoffmann's works, much conflicting evidence can also be adduced. Frequently the "curse of fate" proves to be an excuse by persons who are too weak to master their destiny!

5. Cf. Kenneth Negus, "The Allusions to Schiller's 'Der Geisterseher' in E.T.A. Hoffmann's 'Das Majorat': Meaning and Background," *German Quarterly* 32 (1959): 341–55.

6. See also S, 27, 29, 54–55, 197–98.

7. Walter Müller-Seidel in FN, 767.

8. Cf. Heinisch, "E.T.A. Hoffmann. Die Bergwerke zu Falun," in *Deutsche Romantik*, pp. 134–53.

9. See Georg Ellinger's notes to the "Magnetiseur," W, 15: 159–62; also

Albert Béguin, *L'Ame romantique et le rêve: Essai sur le romantisme allemand et la poésie française* (Paris, 1946).

10. See Marianne Thalmann, "E.T.A. Hoffmanns 'Fräulein von Scuderi,' *Monatshefte* 41 (1949): 107–16; Hellmuth Himmel, "Schuld und Sühne der Scuderi," *MHG* 7 (1960): 1–15; Klaus Kanzog, "E.T.A. Hoffmanns Erzählung 'Das Fräulein von Scuderi' als Kriminalgeschichte," *MHG* 11 (1964): 1–11; J. M. Ellis, "E.T.A. Hoffmann's 'Das Fräulein von Scuderi,'" *Modern Language Review* 64 (1969): 340–50.

Chapter VIII

1. The most outspoken recent criticism of the novel comes from René Wellek, *Midway* 8 (1967): 49–56. Valuable but different evaluations are given by Otmar Schissel von Fleschenberg, *Novellenkomposition in E.T.A. Hoffmanns Elixieren des Teufels* (Halle, 1910); Karl Ochsner, *E.T.A. Hoffmann als Dichter des Unbewussten* (Frauenfeld-Leipzig, 1936); Korff, 4: 572–82; Hewett-Thayer, pp. 250–74; Köhn, pp. 44–90; Segebrecht, *Autobiographie*, pp. 61, 120–99; Taylor, pp. 93 ff.; Karin Cramer, *MHG* 15 (1968): 31–38.

2. It has always been emphasized how difficult it is to comprehend or follow the plot of the novel. Even Walter Müller-Seidel in his otherwise sympathetic evaluation finds: "Aber dass es schwerfällt, in seinen Romanen den Gang der Handlung getreu nachzuzeichnen und nachzuerzählen, erfährt jeder, der es versucht. Selbst durch noch so exakte Stammtafeln genealogischer Art wird die Überschau über das, was in den *Elixieren des Teufels* vor sich geht, nicht wesentlich gefördert. . . . das dergestalt Unübersichtliche in erzählerische Vorzüge umzudeuten, dürfte nicht ohne Gewaltsamkeit möglich sein," *Nachwort*, El, 668. Apparently he refers to Kenneth Negus, "The Family Tree in E.T.A. Hoffmann's *Die Elixiere des Teufels*," *PMLA* 73 (1958): 516–20. The same argument could naturally be advanced for readings of Strindberg, Joyce, or Proust.

3. The reader will be reminded of Ambrosio's spiritual pride in Matthew G. Lewis's *The Monk*. The similarities between the two novels are without genuine significance, although Hoffmann had read *The Monk* before writing his book. Despite John Berryman's claim in his introduction to a new edition of *The Monk* (New York, 1952), p. 13, that "such a work as Thomas Mann's *Doctor Faustus* seems to me frivolous by comparison," Lewis's novel appears already utterly dated in style and conception when compared to the *Devil's Elixirs*.

4. See El, 33, 97–99, 175, 226, 282, 289, and cf. the entries in Hoffmann's diaries, *Tagebücher und literarische Entwürfe*, ed. Hans v. Müller (Berlin, 1915), pp. 6, 71, 100, 105, 110, 126.

5. The views expressed by Medardus presage ideas which Friedrich Nietzsche developed fully in *Jenseits von Gut und Böse* and "Was bedeu-

ten asketische Ideale?" See Friedrich Nietzsche, *Werke*, ed. Karl Schlechta (Munich, 1954–1956), 2: 567–759, 839–900.

6. Many of the characteristics of the psychological novel cited by Leon Edel, *The Modern Psychological Novel* (New York, 1955), pp. 12–23, for example, voyages through consciousness, attempts to retain and record the inwardness of experience, reader having to put the story together, sensations, daydreams, flowing report of thoughts would apply to the *Devil's Elixirs*.

7. See El, 51: "blindly repeating what a strange voice seemed to whisper within me." See also El, 47: ". . . hollow and dull it answered out of me; for I did not speak these words, they escaped my lips involuntarily."

8. This scene is one of several in which violence assumes such proportions that it leaves the reader numb. In discussing the role of the assailant in modern literature, Frederick J. Hoffman, *The Mortal No: Death and the Modern Imagination* (Princeton, 1964), p. 175, raises a question which applies to these scenes. He observes that violence has assumed such magnitude that traditional literary forms can hardly cope with it. Consequently, "language is inadequate to the double task of remaining clearly faithful to its circumstance and at the same time arousing pity and fear in such a way as to effect a purging of these emotions."

9. At first Medardus is also reminded of Aurelie's brother, an association which springs from his fear of insanity. Today's reader will find the Prior's final disclosure incongruous and disappointing. The explanation that Viktorin had survived the fall and in his resulting insanity committed all the crimes envisioned by Medardus was probably intended by Hoffmann to bring the novel back to the established tradition and make it more comprehensible to his contemporaries. Nevertheless, it can only raise new doubts in the reader. But the scene does crystallize the major theme and mirrors once more Medardus's search for the self.

10. The most striking parallels between Medardus's life and the monk's "story" are the following: The monk has an affinity for violence; he demands recognition (El, 106–109) and at times imagines himself to be Saint Anthony (El, 110); he lusts after the forester's girl "in beastly heat," breaks down her door one night and attacks her father with a knife (El, 111); he also suffers from sudden outbursts of remorse which are accompanied by a feeling of abject misery (El, 107); but above all he relates how the devil's elixir has changed his personality (El, 112–13).

11. Medardus's objective at that point resembles Heidegger's "Entschlossenheit zum Mitsein" and is still remote from Buber's "Begegnung auf dem schmalen Grat von Ich und Du."

12. The inserted family history, a chronicle of crimes and incest thriving like weeds, leaves little doubt that the disaster is not fated but the result of the complete negation of reason in favor of violent passion. This thought is developed most clearly when Medardus confronts the Pope:

"The eternal spirit created a giant who can subdue and tame that wild animal that rages in us. The giant is called consciousness and his battle with the animal begets spontaneity. Virtue results from the victory of the giant, sin from the victory of the animal" (El, 248).

Chapter IX

1. Rudolf Eucken, *The Problem of Human Life as Viewed by the Great Thinkers from Plato to the Present Time* (New York, 1914), p. 486.

2. Friedrich Wilhelm Joseph Schelling, *Werke*, ed. M. Schröter (Munich, 1927–1928), 2: 349.

3. See Wilhelm Dilthey, *Grundriss der allgemeinen Geschichte der Philosophie*, ed. Hans-Georg Gadamer (Frankfurt, 1949), p. 218.

bibliography

Allroggen, Gerhard. *E.T.A. Hoffmanns Kompositionen, ein chronologisch-thematisches Verzeichnis seiner musikalischen Werke.* Regensburg: Bosse, 1970.

Beebe, Maurice. *Ivory Towers and Sacred Founts: The Artist as Hero in Fiction from Goethe to Joyce.* New York: New York University Press, 1964.

Binger, Norman H. "Verbal Irony in the Works of E.T.A. Hoffmann." Ph.D. dissertation, Ohio State University, 1942.

Blackmur, Richard P. *The Lion and the Honeycomb. Essays in Solicitude and Critique.* New York: Harcourt, Brace, 1955.

Börne, Ludwig. *Gesammelte Schriften.* Edited by Alfred Klaar. 6 vols. Leipzig: Hesse, 1899.

Bollnow, Otto Friedrich. "Der 'Goldne Topf' und die Naturphilosophie der Romantik." In Bollnow, *Unruhe und Geborgenheit im Weltbild neuerer Dichter*, pp. 207–26. Stuttgart: Kohlhammer, 1953.

Borcherdt, Hans Heinrich. *Der Roman der Goethezeit.* Urach and Stuttgart: Port Verlag, 1949.

Bruning, Peter. "E.T.A. Hoffmann and the Philistine." *German Quarterly* 28 (1955): 111–21.

Buber, Martin. "Urdistanz und Beziehung." In *Werke* 1:411–23. Munich: Kösel, 1962.

Cramer, Thomas. *Das Groteske bei E.T.A. Hoffmann.* Munich: Fink, 1966.

Cronin, John D. "Die Gestalt der Geliebten in den poetischen Werken E.T.A. Hoffmanns." Ph.D. dissertation, University of Bonn, 1967.

Daemmrich, Horst S. "Hoffmann's Tragic Heroes." *Germanic Review* 45 (1970): 94–104.

———. "*The Devil's Elixirs*: Precursor of the Modern Psychological Novel." *Papers on Language and Literature* 6 (1970): 374–86.

———. "Zu E.T.A. Hoffmanns Bestimmung ästhetischer Fragen." *Weimarer Beiträge* 14 (1968): 640–63.

———. "Wirklichkeit als Form: Ein Aspekt Hoffmannscher Erzählkunst." *Colloquia Germanica* 4 (1970): 36–45.

Dilthey, Wilhelm. *Grundriss der allgemeinen Geschichte der Philosophie.* Edited by Hans-Georg Gadamer. Frankfurt: Klostermann, 1949.

Edel, Leon. *The Modern Psychological Novel.* New York: Grove Press, 1955.

Ellis, J. M. "E.T.A. Hoffmann's 'Das Fräulein von Scuderi.'" *Modern Language Review* 64 (1969): 340–50.

Eucken, Rudolf. *The Problem of Human Life as Viewed by the Great Thinkers from Plato to the Present Time.* New York: Scribner's, 1914.

Frey, Marianne. *Der Künstler und sein Werk bei W. H. Wackenroder und E.T.A. Hoffmann.* Bern: Lang & Cie, 1970.

Gloor, Arthur, *E.T.A. Hoffmann. Der Dichter der entwurzelten Geistigkeit.* Zurich: A. G. Fachschriften Verlag, 1947.

Guthke, Karl S. "Der Mythos des Bösen in der westeuropäischen Romantik." *Colloquia Germanica* 2 (1968): 1–36.

Harich, Walter. *E.T.A. Hoffmann. Das Leben eines Künstlers.* 2 vols. Berlin: E. Reiss, 1922.

Heimrich, Bernhard. *Fiktion und Fiktionsironie in Theorie und Dichtung der deutschen Romantik.* Tübingen: Niemeyer, 1968.

Heinisch, Klaus J. *Deutsche Romantik. Interpretationen.* Paderborn: Schöningh, 1966.

Hewett-Thayer, Harvey W. *Hoffmann: Author of the Tales.* Princeton: Princeton University Press, 1948.

Himmel, Hellmuth. "Schuld und Sühne der Scuderi." *Mitteilungen der E.T.A. Hoffmann-Gesellschaft* 7 (1960): 1–15.

Hoffman, Frederick J. *The Mortal No: Death and the Modern Imagination.* Princeton: Princeton University Press, 1964.

Hoffmann, Ernst F. "Zu E.T.A. Hoffmann's 'Sandmann.'" *Monatshefte* 54 (1962): 244–52.

Hoffmann, Ernst Theodor Amadeus. *Werke*. Edited by Georg Ellinger. 15 vols. Berlin: Bong, 1912.

———. *Sämtliche Werke*. Historisch-kritische Ausgabe. Edited by Carl Georg Maassen. Munich: Müller, 1908.

———. *Fantasie- und Nachtstücke*. Edited by Walter Müller-Seidel. Darmstadt: Wissenschaftliche Buchgesellschaft, 1966.

———. *Die Elixiere des Teufels. Lebens-Ansichten des Katers Murr*. Edited by Walter Müller-Seidel. Darmstadt: Wissenschaftliche Buchgesellschaft, 1966.

———. *Die Serapions-Brüder*. Edited by Walter Müller-Seidel. Darmstadt: Wissenschaftliche Buchgesellschaft, 1966.

———. *Späte Werke*. Edited by Walter Müller-Seidel. Darmstadt: Wissenschaftliche Buchgesellschaft, 1966.

———. *Schriften zu Musik. Nachlese*. Edited by Friedrich Schnapp. Darmstadt: Wissenschaftliche Buchgesellschaft, 1966.

———. *E.T.A. Hoffmanns Briefwechsel*. Edited by Friedrich Schnapp. 3 vols. Darmstadt: Wissenschaftliche Buchgesellschaft, 1967–1969.

———. *E.T.A. Hoffmanns Tagebücher und literarische Entwürfe*. Edited by Hans von Müller. Berlin: Paetel, 1915.

Jaffé, Aniela. "Bilder und Symbole aus E.T.A. Hoffmanns Märchen 'Der goldne Topf.'" In Carl G. Jung, *Gestaltungen des Unbewussten*, pp. 239–616. Zurich: Rascher, 1950.

Jauss, Hans Robert. *Die nicht mehr schönen Künste*. Munich: Fink, 1968.

Jebsen, Regine. "Kunstanschauung und Wirklichkeitsbezug bei E.T.A. Hoffmann." Ph.D. dissertation, University of Kiel, 1952.

Jost, Walter. *Von Ludwig Tieck zu E.T.A. Hoffmann. Studien zur Entwicklungsgeschichte des romantischen Subjektivismus*. Frankfurt: Diesterweg, 1921.

Jung, Carl G. *Gestaltungen des Unbewussten*. Zurich: Rascher, 1950.

Kanzog, Klaus. "Grundzüge der E.T.A.-Hoffmann-Forschung seit 1945." *Mitteilungen der E.T.A. Hoffmann-Gesellschaft* 9 (1962): 1–30.

———. "E.T.A. Hoffmann-Literatur 1962–1965. Eine Bibliographie." *Mitteilungen der E.T.A. Hoffmann-Gesellschaft* 12 (1966): 33–38.

———. "E.T.A. Hoffmann-Literatur 1966–1969. Eine Bibliographie." *Mitteilungen der E.T.A. Hoffmann-Gesellschaft* 16 (1970): 28–40.

———. "E.T.A. Hoffmanns Erzählung 'Das Fräulein von Scuderi' als Kriminalgeschichte." *Mitteilungen der E.T.A. Hoffmann-Gesellschaft* 11 (1964): 1–11.

Karoli, Christa. *Ideal und Krise enthusiastischen Künstlertums in der deutschen Romantik.* Bonn: Bouvier, 1968.

Kayser, Wolfgang. *Das Groteske. Seine Gestaltung in Malerei und Dichtung.* Oldenburg: Stalling, 1957.

Köhn, Lothar. *Vieldeutige Welt.* Tübingen: Niemeyer, 1966.

Köpp, Klaus F. "Realismus in E.T.A. Hoffmanns Erzählung 'Prinzessin Brambilla.'" *Weimarer Beiträge* 12 (1966): 51–80.

Kohlschmidt, Werner. "Nihilismus der Romantik." In Kohlschmidt, *Form und Innerlichkeit. Beiträge zur Geschichte und Wirkung der deutschen Klassik und Romantik,* pp. 157–76. Bern: Francke, 1955.

Korff, Hermann August. *Geist der Goethezeit.* Vol. 4: 582–91. Leipzig: Koehler & Amelang, 1964.

Kreplin, Dietrich. "Das Automaten-Motiv bei E.T.A. Hoffmann." Ph.D. dissertation, University of Bonn, 1957.

Langen, August. "Deutsche Sprachgeschichte vom Barock bis zur Gegenwart." In *Deutsche Philologie im Aufriss,* 2nd ed., 1: 1252–57. Berlin: Schmidt, 1952–1957.

Loevenich, Heinz. "Einheit und Symbolik des Kater Murr. Zur Einführung in Hoffmanns Roman." *Der Deutschunterricht* 16, no. 2 (1964): 72–86.

McClain, William H. "E.T.A. Hoffmann as a Psychological Realist. A Study of 'Meister Floh.'" *Monatshefte* 47 (1955): 65–80.

Marquard, Odo. "Zur Bedeutung der Theorie des Unbewussten für eine Theorie der nicht mehr schönen Kunst." In Jauss, *Die nicht mehr schönen Künste,* pp. 375–92.

Martini, Fritz. "Die Märchendichtungen E.T.A. Hoffmanns." *Der Deutschunterricht* 7, no. 2 (1955): 56–78.

Meyer, Herman. *Das Zitat in der Erzählkunst.* Stuttgart: Metzler, 1961.

Mollenauer, Robert. "The Three Periods of E.T.A. Hoffmann's Romanticism: An Attempt at a Definition." *Studies in Romanticism* 2 (1963): 213–43.

Mühlher, Robert. "Die Einheit der Künste und das Orphische bei E.T.A. Hoffmann." In *Stoffe, Formen, Strukturen,* edited by Albert Fuchs and Helmut Motekat, pp. 345–60. Munich: Hueber, 1962.

———. "Ernst Theodor Amadeus Hoffmann. Beiträge zu einer Motiv-Interpretation." *Literaturwissenschaftliches Jahrbuch der Görres-Gesellschaft* N.F. 4 (1963): 55–72.

———. "E.T.A. Hoffmann und das Spätbarock." *Jahrbuch des Wiener Goethe-Vereins* 67 (1963): 139–52.

———. "Liebestod und Spiegelmythe in Hoffmanns Märchen 'Der

goldne Topf.' " In Mühlher, *Dichtung der Krise*, pp. 43–95. Vienna: Herold, 1951.

―――. "Prinzessin Brambilla. Ein Beitrag zum Verständnis der Dichtung." *Mitteilungen der E.T.A. Hoffmann-Gesellschaft* 5 (1958): 5–24.

Müller, Dieter. "Zeit der Automate. Zum Automatenproblem bei Hoffmann." *Mitteilungen der E.T.A. Hoffmann-Gesellschaft* 12 (1966): 1–10.

Müller, Helmut. *Untersuchungen zum Problem der Formelhaftigkeit bei E.T.A. Hoffmann*. Bern: Haupt, 1964.

Negus, Kenneth. "The Allusions to Schiller's 'Der Geisterseher' in E.T.A. Hoffmann's 'Das Majorat': Meaning and Background." *German Quarterly* 32 (1959): 341–55.

―――. *E.T.A. Hoffmann's Other World*. Philadelphia: University of Pennsylvania Press, 1965.

―――. "The Family Tree in E.T.A. Hoffmann's *Die Elixiere des Teufels*." *PMLA* 73 (1958): 516–20.

―――. "Thematic Structures in Three Major Works of E.T.A. Hoffmann." Ph.D. dissertation, University of Princeton, 1957.

Nietzsche, Friedrich. *Werke*. Edited by Karl Schlechta. 3 vols. Munich: Hanser, 1954–1956.

Ochsner, Karl. *E.T.A. Hoffmann als Dichter des Unbewussten*. Frauenfeld-Leipzig: Huber & Co., 1936.

Ohl, Hubert. "Der reisende Enthusiast. Studien zur Haltung des Erzählers in den 'Fantasiestücken' E.T.A. Hoffmanns." Ph.D. dissertation, University of Frankfurt, 1955.

Passage, Charles E. *The Russian Hoffmannists*. The Hague: Mouton, 1963.

Paulsen, Wolfgang, ed. *Das Nachleben der Romantik in der modernen deutschen Literatur*. Heidelberg: Stiehm, 1969.

Peckham, Morse. *Beyond the Tragic Vision. The Quest for Identity in the Nineteenth Century*. New York: Braziller, 1962.

―――. *Man's Rage for Chaos. Biology, Behavior, and the Arts*. Philadelphia: Chilton, 1965.

Planta, Urs Orlando von. *E.T.A. Hoffmanns Märchen "Das fremde Kind."* Bern: Francke, 1958.

Prawer, S. S. "Hoffmann's Uncanny Guest: A Reading of *Der Sandmann*." *German Life and Letters* 18 (1965): 297–308.

Praz, Mario. *The Romantic Agony*. New York: Meridian, 1956.

Preisendanz, Wolfgang. "Eines matt geschliffnen Spiegels dunkler Widerschein." In *Festschrift für Jost Trier zum 70. Geburtstag*. Edited by William Foerste and Karl Heinz Borck, pp. 411–29. Cologne: Böhlau, 1964.

———. *Humor als dichterische Einbildungskraft. Studien zur Erzählkunst des poetischen Realismus*. Munich: Eidos, 1963.

Rehm, Walther. *Der Todesgedanke in der deutschen Dichtung vom Mittelalter bis zur Romantik*. Halle: Niemeyer, 1928.

Ricci, Jean-F.-A. *E.T.A. Hoffmann. L'homme et l'oeuvre*. Paris: Corti, 1947.

Rockenbach, Klaus. "Bauformen romantischer Kunstmärchen. Eine Studie zur epischen Integration des Wunderbaren bei E.T.A. Hoffmann." Ph.D. dissertation, University of Bonn, 1957.

Rosen, Robert. *E.T.A. Hoffmanns "Kater Murr." Aufbauformen und Erzählsituationen*. Bonn: Bouvier, 1970.

Rosteutscher, Joachim. *Das ästhetische Idol im Werke von Winckelmann, Novalis, Hoffmann, Goethe, George und Rilke*. Bern: Francke, 1956.

Sander, Volkmar. "Realität und Bewusstsein bei E.T.A. Hoffmann." In *Studies in Germanic Languages and Literature*. Presented to Professor E.A.G. Rose. Edited by Robert Fowkes and Volkmar Sander, pp. 115–26. New York: New York University, 1967.

Scher, Steven Paul. *Verbal Music in German Literature*. New Haven: Yale University Press, 1968.

Schelling, Friedrich Wilhelm Joseph. *Werke*. Edited by M. Schröter. 6 vols. Munich: Beck, 1927–1928.

Schiller, Johann Christoph Friedrich. *Sämtliche Werke*. Edited by Eduard von der Hellen. 16 vols. Stuttgart: Cotta, 1904–1905.

Schissel von Fleschenberg, Otmar. *Novellenkomposition in E.T.A. Hoffmanns Elixieren des Teufels*. Halle: Niemeyer, 1910.

Schütz, Christel. "Studien zur Erzählkunst E.T.A. Hoffmanns." Ph.D. dissertation, University of Göttingen, 1955.

Schultz, Franz. *Klassik und Romantik der Deutschen*, 3rd ed., 2 vols. Stuttgart: Metzler, 1959.

Segebrecht, Wulf. *Autobiographie und Dichtung. Eine Studie zum Werk E.T.A. Hoffmanns*. Stuttgart: Metzler, 1967.

———. "E.T.A. Hoffmanns Auffassung vom Richteramt und vom Dichterberuf. Mit unbekannten Zeugnissen aus Hoffmanns juristischer Tätigkeit." *Jahrbuch der deutschen Schillergesellschaft* 11 (1967): 62–138.

———. "Hoffmanns Todesdarstellungen. *Mitteilungen der E.T.A. Hoffmann-Gesellschaft* 12 (1966): 11–19.

Singer, Herbert. "E.T.A. Hoffmann. *Kater Murr.*" In *Der deutsche Roman vom Barock bis zur Gegenwart.* Edited by Benno von Wiese, 1: 301–28. Düsseldorf: Bagel, 1963.

Strohschneider-Kohrs, Ingrid. *Die romantische Ironie in Theorie und Gestaltung.* Tübingen: Niemeyer, 1960.

Tauber, Serge. "Die Bedeutung der künstlichen Menschenfigur im Werke E.T.A. Hoffmanns." Ph.D. dissertation, University of Innsbruck, 1960.

Taylor, Ronald. *Hoffmann.* London: Bowes & Bowes, 1963.

Terras, Victor. "E.T.A. Hoffmanns polyphonische Erzählkunst." *German Quarterly* 39 (1966): 549–69.

Thalmann, Marianne. "E.T.A. Hoffmann's 'Fräulein von Scuderi.'" *Monatshefte* 41 (1949): 107–16.

———. *Das Märchen und die Moderne.* Stuttgart: Kohlhammer, 1961.

———. *Romantik und Manierismus.* Stuttgart: Kohlhammer, 1963.

———. *Der Trivialroman des 18. Jahrhunderts und der romantische Roman.* Berlin: Ebering, 1923.

———. *Zeichensprache der Romantik.* Heidelberg: Stiehm, 1967.

———. *The Literary Sign Language of German Romanticism.* Translated by Harold A. Basilius. Detroit: Wayne State University Press, 1972.

Tretter, Friedrich Giseller. "Die Frage nach der Wirklichkeit bei E.T.A. Hoffmann." Ph.D. dissertation, University of Munich, 1961.

Wiese, Benno von. *Die deutsche Novelle von Goethe bis Kafka.* 2 vols. Düsseldorf: Bagel, 1960–1962.

———. *Von Lessing bis Grabbe. Studien zur deutschen Klassik und Romantik.* Düsseldorf: Bagel, 1968.

Wöllner, Günter. *E.T.A. Hoffmann und Franz Kafka. Von der "fortgeführten Metapher" zum "sinnlichen Paradox."* Sprache und Dichtung 20. Bern: Haupt, 1971.

Ziolkowski, Theodor. "Das Nachleben der Romantik in der modernen deutschen Literatur. Methodologische Überlegungen." In *Das Nachleben der Romantik in der modernen deutschen Literatur,* edited by Wolfgang Paulsen, pp. 15–31. Heidelberg: Stiehm, 1969.

index

Alter ego projections, 22, 74, 98–99, 101–2, 104

Art, 20, 27, 42–43, 47, 51, 61, 65, 66–67, 71, 74, 113–14

Artistic creation, 26, 27, 29–30, 32–37, 40–46

Artists, 26–37, 39–46, 47, 66–67, 87–88, 117

Baudelaire, Charles, 18

Blood, 23, 101–2, 105, 106, 116

Börne, Ludwig, 17

Bonaventura, 22, 111

Bouterwek, Friedrich, 114–15

Brentano, Clemens, 14

Cage, 9, 30–31, 40, 46, 51, 61–62, 78, 79, 98, 103, 104, 109, 116

Chamisso, Adalbert von, 15, 17, 77

Criticism of society and man's spiritual decline, 20, 23, 27–28, 40–41, 43, 46, 64–66, 68–69, 74, 75, 87–88

Delibes, Clément Léo, 16

Devrient, Ludwig, 14, 15

Eichendorff, Joseph von, 17

Evil, 22–23, 48, 59, 73–74, 79, 86–89, 98–99, 103, 105–6

Eye, 25, 47–50, 96, 116

Faulkner, William, 74

Fear, 9, 23, 40, 45, 48–51, 57, 60–61, 74, 75, 79, 84–85, 89, 96–97, 101, 116

Fichte, Johann Gottlieb, 15, 112

Flame, circle of, 25, 49–50

Fouqué, Friedrich de la Motte, 15, 17

Goethe, Johann Wolfgang von, 17, 18, 111

Grand design, 9, 10, 23, 46, 56–57, 59–62, 64, 65–66, 70–71, 73–75, 78, 80–81, 83, 85, 86–87, 106–7, 109, 116–18

Harsányi, Tibor, 16
Hausegger, Siegmund von, 16
Hebbel, Friedrich, 17
Hegel, Georg Wilhelm Friedrich, 112
Heine, Heinrich, 17
Hindemith, Paul, 16
Hippel, Theodor, 14
Hoffmann, Ernst Theodor Amadeus,
  "The Artus Exchange," 32, 34, 35, 37
  "Automata," 73, 75–76
  "The Contest of the Minstrels," 87–88
  "Councilor Krespel," 47, 51–53
  "The Cousin's Corner Window," 27, 37, 46
  "The Dei von Elbe in Paris," 117
  The Devil's Elixirs, 17, 22, 41, 93–107
  "Don Juan," 26–27, 52–53
  "The Enemy," 37
  "Gambler's Luck," 16, 85, 93, 107–9
  "Gluck," 15, 25–26, 37
  The Golden Pot, 22, 28–32, 66
  "Ignaz Denner," 73, 85, 87
  "Jaques Callot," 27, 46
  "The Jesuit Church in G.," 32–33, 34
  Kreisleriana, 27, 33–34, 39–40, 41–42, 43, 45, 88
  Life and Opinions of Tomcat Murr, 22, 27, 28, 34, 39–46
  Little Zaches Called Zinnober, 55, 64–66, 71
  "Mademoiselle de Scudéry," 73, 85, 87–91
  "The Magnetizer," 85–87, 100
  Master Flea, 16, 22, 50, 55, 67–71
  "The Mines of Falun," 73, 78, 83–85
  Musical compositions, 15, 16

  "The Mysterious Child," 55, 56, 62–64
  "The Mystery of the Deserted House," 81
  "A New Year's Eve Adventure," 34, 76–78
  Nutcracker and the King of Mice, 28, 55–62, 117
  "The Primogeniture," 78–81
  Princess Brambilla, 66–67, 71
  "The Sandman," 34, 47–51
  "Signor Formica," 35
  The Serapion Brethren, 17, 36–37, 46, 56, 87
  "The Story of the Lost Reflection," *see* "A New Year's Eve Adventure"
  "The Vow," 73, 78, 81–83

Infernal fairy tale, 80–81, 83, 88, 116

Jean Paul (Richter), 17, 22

Kant, Immanuel, 112
Kleist, Heinrich von, 82
Kósa, György, 16

MacLeish, Archibald, 37
Malipiero, Gian Francesco, 16
Marionettes, 48–50, 51, 57–58, 60, 61–62, 64, 70, 75–76, 116
Mark (Marc), Julia, 15, 34
Mozart, 53

Nature, 20, 25, 29–30, 33, 35, 41–42, 50, 62–63, 65, 67, 69, 84, 99
Novalis (Hardenberg, Friedrich von), 14

Offenbach, Jacques, 16

Rangström, Ture, 17
Reality and transcendental vision, 19, 20, 21, 23, 30–31, 35–36, 55–56, 58, 62, 64, 73, 74, 82

Scott, Sir Walter, 17

Schleiermacher, Friedrich, 15

Schelling, Friedrich, 112–14

Schopenhauer, Arthur, 115–16

Schubert, Gotthilf Heinrich, 114

Schiller, Friedrich, 79, 111

Schütt, Eduard, 16

Schumann, Robert A., 16

Sekles, Bernhard, 17

Self-realization, 9, 22, 25–26, 56, 57, 59, 61–62, 67, 68, 69–71, 73, 78, 84, 86, 93, 105–7, 115, 117

Self-transcendence, 9, 25–26, 33, 40, 52–53, 57, 64, 94, 105–6, 116

Shattered self, 22–23, 41, 47, 56, 75, 77, 81, 82–83, 89, 94–99, 100, 101–7, 108, 109, 118

Spontini, Gasparo, 16

Stylistic patterns, 20, 21, 23, 30–32, 44, 47, 51, 55, 56–58, 64, 67, 73–75, 76, 78, 79–81, 83, 88–89, 93–94, 96, 98, 102–3, 106–7, 116

Swift, Jonathan, 65

Tchaikovsky, Peter, 16, 61

Tieck, Ludwig, 14, 17, 64

Virgin and vampire, 34–35, 42, 76–78, 81, 99, 108

Weigel, Joseph, 16

Will to power, 23, 26–27, 86–88, 94, 96–98, 100–1, 104, 105, 115

Horst S. Daemmrich is professor of German at Wayne State University. He received his B.A. and M.A. degrees from Wayne State University and his Ph.D. degree from the University of Chicago. Among his writings is *The Challenge of German Literature* (1971), which he edited with Diether Haenicke and which was published by the Wayne State University Press.

The manuscript was edited by Marguerite C. Wallace. The book was designed by Don Ross. The typeface for the text is Linotype Caledonia designed by W. A. Dwiggins about 1938; and the display faces include Futura light and Umbra chapter number.

The text is printed on Nashoba paper and the book is bound in Columbia Mills' Fictionette Natural finish cloth over binders' boards. Manufactured in the United States of America.